ENDINGS & BEGINNINGS:
FAMILY ESSAYS

Praise for *Endings & Beginnings*

In these superb essays, DeWitt Henry shows himself to be a master of the form. Whether he is writing about his life-long experience as a golfer or with guns or having grown up in the shadow of privilege and alcoholism, one senses that Henry is stepping nakedly, and with a clear and unsentimental eye, into the abiding mystery of the decades of his life thus far: as a son, a brother, a husband and father, a writer, a teacher, a friend. But he accomplishes all this without trying to solve that mystery but to simply live it. This is not an easy path, but perhaps it is the only path toward wisdom, which is abundant in this moving, deeply compelling, and indispensable collection. *Endings & Beginnings: Family Essays* is a gem. —Andre Dubus III, author of *Townie*

When DeWitt Henry writes that "our games rehearsed our lives," I nodded: so true; well said. As I continued reading, it occurred to me that the most dramatic moments (terrible illness; how loved ones are lost; the difficulties of parenting) also rehearse our lives, and are also only a dress rehearsal. How many people get their big moment on the stage, and if so, for how long? This is the writer's implied question throughout. Maybe it's better to resist the usual tendency to extrapolate from accounts of other people's lives in order to better understand our own, and to simply read them as individual statements that point inward, to the heart of an individual. These would be good essays with which to start.
—Ann Beattie, author of *A Wonderful Stroke of Luck*

With *Endings & Beginnings: Family Essays,* we have a book filled with the kinds of secrets all of our families hide but almost never reveal. DeWitt Henry proves himself to be the honest, frank, and skilled chronicler of many lives, recounting the moving histories of his own parents, siblings, and children. We are the fortunate ones as readers to be able to share in the telling of these stories, because by the end what we also learn is Henry's own story as a son, father, husband, and writer; indeed, he is vulnerable, sensitive, making connections we might not realize, confessing his own fears and limitations, with a rare admirable humility.
—Allen Gee, author of *My Chinese America*

Henry is a fascinating man, made of fascinating stock and pursuits: his family's chocolate business; his once obsession with golf; his father's "bad years"; the challenges of parenting and marriage; the betrayals of colleagues and friends; familial bonds. I was very impressed, in fact, at how unsentimentally yet lovingly he writes of his family, especially his brothers, though perhaps the greatest praise I can give is that he made me wish I had grown up appreciating guns and gun culture. "Embodiment" opened a window into his humanity and I thought it was a particularly brave essay, and, with "Father of the Bride," (notwithstanding his hysterically awkward mention of Colombian weed) the collection ended on the perfect notes of love, bonds, and hope.

—Jerald Walker, author of *How To Make A Slave*

Endings & Beginnings is a stirring distillation of what it means to be connected—whether through life-long rituals of golf and swimming, or the more monumental of weddings and family losses. As well as through the *things* of our lives; Henry recalls the BB pistols of not only his own childhood, but of his son's, when he sets up a makeshift range in his office to shoot at cartoon targets; then of his dying brother teaching his son how to shoot another gun he remembers. The careful refining of such moments into, as Henry describes, "a wholeness to the landscape in which I live," is the driving power behind this keenly thoughtful and at turns, humorous and haunting new collection.

—Sandra Tyler, author of *Blue Glass*

Earlier praise for *Safe Suicide*

Elegantly written, edgy, touching, inventive, surprising in its shifts of style and form, and completely spellbinding from start to finish, this is a book that works its way under your skin and down into your vital organs. —Tim O'Brien, author of *Dad's Maybe Book*

Henry's family story is enriched by his ardent investigations, by his prose and his telling, or tellings, as each essay in memoir prompts more.
—David Hamilton, author of *A Certain Arc*

Safe Suicide is held together by Henry's searching voice, his attempts to do the right thing even when it's difficult. The book's trajectory shows him growing into manhood, finding love, work, and a family that gives his life meaning. After describing his journey, Henry ends on a humble note of grace: "Life itself is our glory and ordeal, our measure of heart, and passion. We do our best." —Chuck Leddy, *The Boston Globe*

Earlier praise for *Sweet Dreams*

A wonderful account of a family, a period, and a young man by a writer who depicts with fearless precision his own longings, flaws, and remarkable gifts. —Margot Livesey, author of *The Boy in the Field*

Sweet Dreams is a coming-of-age book. It is a book about the boy who grew up with candy wealth, fell in love with a toy printing press, and decided, early on, to be a Writer. One can decide to be a Writer, but the world, in some ways, has to stand equal to that dream. It's a contest of wills, or it can be seen as one, and DeWitt takes us through the bruises and glories. He dreams out loud. We're there.
—Beth Kephart, author of *Strike the Empty*

ENDINGS & BEGINNINGS:
FAMILY ESSAYS

DeWitt Henry

MadHat Press
Cheshire, Massachusetts

MadHat Press
MadHat Incorporated
PO Box 422, Cheshire, MA 01225

Copyright © 2021 DeWitt Henry
All rights reserved

The Library of Congress has assigned
this edition a Control Number of
2020952597

ISBN 978-1-952335-16-7 (paperback)

Text by DeWitt Henry
Cover design by Marc Vincenz
Cover image: M.C. Escher's "Bond of Union"© 2020 The M.C.
Escher Company—The Netherlands. All rights reserved.
www.mcescher.com

www.madhat-press.com

First Printing

Also by DeWitt Henry

Sweet Marjoram: Notes and Essays, 2018 (essays)

Falling: Six Stories, 2016 (fiction)

Visions of a Wayne Childhood, 2012 (memoir)

Sweet Dreams: A Family History, 2011 (memoir)

Safe Suicide: Essays, Narratives, and Meditations, 2008 (memoir)

The Marriage of Anna Maye Potts, 2001 (novel)

Sorrow's Company: Writers on Loss and Grief, 2001 (editor)

Breaking Into Print: Early Stories and Insights into Getting Published: A Ploughshares anthology, 2000 (editor)

Fathering Daughters: Reflections by Men, 1998 (co-editor with James Alan McPherson)

Other Sides of Silence: New Fiction from Ploughshares, 1993 (editor)

The Ploughshares Reader: New Fiction for the Eighties, 1984 (editor)

For my granddaughters, Eva, Maya, and Olivia

On a huge hill,
Cragged and steep, Truth stands, and he that will
Reach her, about must, and about must go;
And what the hill's suddenness resists, win so.

—John Donne, Satire III: On Religion

Table of Contents

Introduction by John Skoyles   xiii

On Golf (2007)   1
Perspectives (2003)   15
Deaths in My Life (1994)   25
Embodiment (1995)   33
Looking Through the Knothole (2010)   39
Long Distance (1998)   61
Swimming (2003)   85
Guns in My Life (2004)   89
Father of the Bride (2008)   127

Acknowledgments   147
About the Author   149

Introduction

Endings and Beginnings: Family Essays marks the third and concluding volume of DeWitt Henry's trilogy, a work that began with *Sweet Dreams, A Family History* and extended to *Safe Suicide: Narratives, Essays, and Meditations.*

In Henry's world, *Family* is not restricted to the household of his parents, siblings and extended relatives. A graceful writer of tremendous compassion, Henry sees all lives as interconnected and each of his essays breaks the boundaries of its original impulse. The resulting collections often focus on family at the start, but reach well beyond, and have an appealing sweep of understanding of all walks of life.

Sweet Dreams vividly captured Henry's early years growing up near Philadelphia, and his childhood had a sweet background indeed: his grandfather (after whom he is named) owned a chocolate factory. The reminiscences, however, are not all sugary: his alcoholic father loomed large over the household, with young DeWitt, even at the young age of nine, understanding the transformation that booze makes in an individual. He equated his father with Lon Chaney in *The Wolfman,* watching his father become a monster as he drank. This first book shows us the author as the enterprising and indefatigable publisher/editor/printer of his fourth-grade newsletter, foreshadowing his founding of a renowned literary journal decades later. It takes us through Amherst, Harvard, Iowa and ends with the death of his parents, the birth of a daughter and adoption of a son.

Safe Suicide focuses in dramatic detail on some of the events discussed generally in the first volume, but also goes beyond that book in depth and range. It delves perceptively into the father's alcoholism; provides an extraordinarily sensual and heart-breaking account of the author's sister, 19, exposing herself to him at 13 to satisfy his curiosity about the opposite sex, and relates the history of the founding of *Ploughshares,* a story of literary entrepreneurship and editorial genius that shows the state of not only the literary world, but of American culture. The explorations of a writer mid-life include bungee-jumping, becoming aroused during a therapeutic massage, running the Boston Marathon, losing close friends (including the poet Bill Knott), and admiring a daughter's accomplishments as a visual artist.

Both of the earlier volumes concerned themselves with beginning and endings, and they are noted in a way that is enlightening: we begin to see the world in these terms, something that does not end after the books are put away: the vision lingers, strong and true with an appreciation of life's stops and starts.

The present collection, *Endings and Beginnings: Family Essays,* focuses directly on initiations and conclusions, and such an intense scrutiny makes for the most powerful book of the three. Perceptive, humorous in the most self-deprecating ways (a trip to a golf course with author Tim O'Brien depicts our out-of-practice narrator's first drive resulting in the head of the club flying off the shaft and traveling farther than the ball …). We recall a Mr. Young, back at Henry's home course, dapper at 94, his golf-playing days over, spending his time on the putting green…. And Henry, no longer in his former form, still manages to pass his love of the game to his son and, later, to his granddaughter. Such are the pleasures of the opening essay, "On Golf," which is about much more than a game of sport.

Other essays provide a fascinating history of the Henry clan's fortunes in business, as his father left the candy factory to take a position with their chocolate supplier, Walker Baker Company, as "General Assistant on Coating and Cocoa Producing," in Dorchester, Massachusetts. At the height of a successful career there, his father moved back to Pennsylvania to rescue the family company from the brink of ruin. As the story is told, one cannot but marvel at the tale being spun amid signposts such as a brass plaque on the factory door announcing *DeWitt P. Henry, Confectioners,* the name of the grandfather and of our author/narrator. The move back into the family arms and business propels Henry's father into a severe struggle with alcoholism, a harrowing tale of his out-of-control drinking, an affair with a young woman at the factory, and his eventual recovery and sale of the company to Pet Foods, owner of Whitman's Chocolates. The account is riveting, rife with details such as the patriarch's favorite song being, "Looking through the Knothole of Father's Wooden Leg," with its bizarre lyrics:

> A horsey stood around
> with his feet upon the ground.

Oh, who will wind the clock
When I am gone?
Go get the ax,
There's a fly on Lizzie's ear.
And a boy's best friend is his mother.

… which Henry makes sense of, noting that, "only by seeing through your father's weakness and by admitting to his humanity can you claim your life." And so, we too, as readers, peer through this lens.

Alcoholism runs in the Henry family, and its investigation in these essays is heartfelt, powerful and true. A portrait of Chuck, Henry's surgeon brother, deals with this issue in a moving way. The favorite doctor-son of the parents, who has been held up as a model by his parents to our narrator, he fathers three sons who are plagued by the disease. Henry becomes executor of his brother's will, and survives what is a complex of relationships and difficult choices.

Much of this collection is a truly disconcerting look at mortality. He writes, "And then it comes. Your ending." But the author's rumination on his own "ending" is not self-absorbed; his essays recount his deep friendship with Richard Yates, his family ties, and those relationships that developed over his career as teacher, writer, administrator and editor. There is a wistfulness that contains not an iota of regret, but allows the reader to understand the life as registered, also permitting the reader to look at his own life. The piece "Deaths in My Life" is really about "the people in my life," as Henry's nephew, John Friedericy, a painter and sculptor, has titled one of his paintings. The account of his battle with AIDS exemplifies the scope of Henry's method: the angle is intensely personal and the result is entirely universal.

Through all of these reminiscences: a swim that returns love to a marriage; a history of handling guns that gets his son in trouble although the weapon is a toy, and a daughter's giving birth, there is one uplifting, unifying constant: the narrator, a person who endures, who takes responsibility, who stands up for what is right without being righteous, and who is kind to the bone. A person who believes that a moment of strife might very well transform into an hour, a day, a week, or a lifetime of survival and peace. In *Endings and Beginnings,* our guide becomes our

DeWitt Henry

companion, someone we wished we had known in the flesh. And by the end of this collection, we have done so. Whitman's words are apt here: *This is no book; Who touches this, touches a man.*

—John Skoyles

On Golf

Golf was as central to my childhood's family in the 1950s as swimming, writing, drawing and painting, or the candy factory that my grandfather had started and that my father now ran.

There were always golf clubs, golf bags, golf balls, putters, whiffle golf balls, rubber targets for putting on rugs, golf shoes with cleats, fingerless golf gloves, and green sun visors around our house, mostly in the downstairs closet (a huge closet, where umbrellas, overcoats, Dad's felt hats and Mom's special silver fox stole and its fox-head clasp hung). There were also trophies from past tournaments, a crystal dish for cigarettes with a silver lid; three or four crystal ashtrays with silver rims; a silver cup with winged handles; a golden figurine of a golfer on a wooden base, with a little plaque. Mom, Chuck and Dad practiced their swings outside, drove whiffle balls and hit chip shots in the side yard, careful not to take divots.

Jack and Judy never played. Jack was absorbed by his cars and by hunting, Judy by swimming and reading. Chuck had been Junior Club Champion, and several of the ashtrays were his. He had his own set of clubs, his own golf shoes.

My mother's financier father, Jerome Thralls, had played on Long Island, and when my mother was a teenager she had walked the course with him. The St. Davids Golf Club, where we had our family membership, had once been the pasture of my great-grandfather Henry's dairy farm. In fact, the very house in which my father had been born stood behind the tenth-hole green. When my great-grandfather had died, the farm had been sold by my grandfather, so that they could buy the Bloomingdale Avenue house in Wayne, and he could continue to build his candy business in Philadelphia.

In our home movies, a younger, leaner Dad practices swings at Bloomingdale, before and after I was born. He had started playing in Boston, when he worked for the Walter Baker Company. They had moved back home from Boston after my grandfather's heart attack, and been given the family house, while my grandparents moved first to a farm in Malvern, and then to their retirement house in Ithan. His swings were always a strange chopping scoop at the ball, and then he would fall away because of his bad leg.

Mom (I was told by Mom) used to be really good. Some of the trophies were hers. She had her bag, her golf shoes, and her good set of ladies' clubs. But shortly before we moved from Bloomingdale to St. Davids, during Dad's "bad time," she and her clubs went alone on a golfing vacation to Bermuda, where she says she "played until there was nothing else." But then after we moved she had bursa problems—calcium deposits, in her shoulder, arm—and after operations on them was left so weakened that she doubted if she could ever play again. Her swing had stiffened. She began to take lessons. She played with a ladies' foursome on ladies' day.

Our family club membership included a monthly dining room charge whether we ate there or not. So periodically, on Sundays, Dad would "take us out to eat," and after my grandfather's death, sometimes brought Nana Henry as well. Except for Mom, we all hated this; hated the dressing up, and the stiff formality. Dad called the middle-aged waiter by name, Tony, and Tony welcomed him personally as Mr. Henry, and then Mom, Mrs. Henry, and smiled at us admiringly, the Henrys. In summers, our table was on a porch with open screened windows that overlooked the putting green and vistas of the fifth, eighth and ninth fairways. As we ordered, I watched distant players with envy, wishing I could be out there (in shorts, tee shirt and golf shoes, carrying my bag), instead of here (in my suit with scratchy pants, my shirt with starched collar, my white buck shoes). When Mom ordered, she always said "the": "I'll have the lamb." Chuck and

Jack went for steak; Dad, Judy and I for roast beef "au jus," pink in the center and crisp brown at the borders. Dinners at the club were one of our few public appearances as a family (another was Christmas Eve or Easter services at the Wayne Presbyterian Church). Dad and Mom greeted other members with a smile or nod, or sometimes people came over to say hello, and we all were introduced.

One branch of the club's activities involved junior members, the teenaged children of adult members, for whom tournaments and lessons, as well as social activities, were arranged.

Chuck had been Junior Champion, renowned for his long drives and iron shots. I remember one of our first family foursomes—or maybe it was only an early occasion when I walked around with the three of them, or caddied for my mother—and our marveling at the distance and accuracy of Chuck's shots. The fact that he could possibly reach the greens of the long par fours in two shots seemed to me a kind of magic, inimitable. His ball would lift clean and high in the air, and keep going, beyond what any of us could expect or believe.

When I turned thirteen, I began to go to the junior clinics and to play in their nine-hole tournaments, which were held on Sunday afternoons. Both Mom and Dad had taken regular lessons from Tommy, the club pro. Now in the junior clinics, Tommy checked my grip. He said I had a natural swing. Keep my eye on the ball, head fixed. Slow back swing, along the line of flight, then swivel hips, head down, and follow through.

At first, I played with hand-me-down clubs. Some had been Grandpop Thralls's, some Mom's (Dad had bought her a new set), or Dad's or Chuck's. I wore Dad's castaway shoes. Later, as I got more serious, I saved up money from odd jobs to buy new Spaulding Irons, one by one; and as Dad's old woods decayed, a Ben Hogan driver. I won the drawing for a new bag at a candy manufacturers' convention we attended with Dad.

The golf club was a realm unto itself, apart from my public-high-school world (in fact, most club juniors went to private school). Where football or basketball might lead to popularity at school, golf was strictly a personal, or a family thing.

3

Only three or four of families from my public school belonged to St. Davids, including the Kings, and Dave King was my only classmate to play golf. Taller than I was, "Kingy" was starting center on our basketball team (where I didn't make the team), starting right end in football (where I was third-string center), and a mainstay in track for hurdles and the 440 (where I filled in for field events). At school he was friendly, though never a friend. At the club, aside from a chance practice round, we never played together. He established himself as Junior Champion, and usually played with Tommy (the pro), Bobby Lenniger (the former Junior Champion after Chuck), or adult members with low handicaps. He even went on to hold the Club Championship for several years in a row, starting in 11th grade. At the club he was a personage, but golf meant nothing to his friends at school.

Another classmate, Dick Curley, showed up to caddy, and that troubled me—here he was Sally Yerkes's boyfriend, a hearty, well-liked starter, like King, in all the sports. I knew that his family was poor, but I didn't want him to see me here as a member's son. I didn't want him caddying for my family, watching and knowing us that way.

Once I'd begun to break 50 for nine holes, playing with my fellow juniors, Chuck agreed to take me out to play full rounds, becoming both my mentor and my rival. He came and went during these years, first dropping out of Cornell, then starting at Franklin and Marshall, then drafted and serving in Korea, then home again and in medical school at Hahnemann.

For several summers, I became a club rat. Before I got my license, Mom or Chuck would drop me off, and pick me up later. The shag bag and balls were in Dad's locker, which Walter, the aging black attendant, opened for me. As I changed into golf shoes, Walter took my street loafers without asking and shined them, then return them to the locker. Rarely, but sometimes, other adult members were changing. They greeted me as Dad's son.

Unless adults were practicing or having a lesson, I hit practice nine-irons to the practice green. Sometimes, I paid a caddy $10 to shag practice drives and long irons from the shade of a tree beside the first tee, out over the 18th and 17th fairways. Members golfing hated this, of course, since, as they played, their own ball might be hard to find among the practice balls. But I would practice, practice, priding myself on my long ball, which was straight most of the time, but otherwise sent my caddy running. I spent hours as well on the putting green, making way for Mr. Young, who was 94, dapper, and who drove a 30-year-old black sedan at no more than 15 mph, and spent his entire day putting.

Gradually, my game improved. I could make some pars and even some birdies, along with all the bogies and double bogies. I played full rounds regularly with two other juniors, who were younger than me, and neither as good; and some days, even two rounds. I played in tournaments, never placing at the top, but sometimes coming close. But all that was put to the test in our family threesomes and foursomes.

Dad's own game was stable. He played every week with his Saturday foursome, as he had been for years. Overweight, and with his bad leg, he put in his five-day executive week; then disappeared early Saturday morning in slacks, loafers, and a polo shirt. He'd return in mid-afternoon, then fall into a deep sleep on our living room couch. If for any reason, he missed a Saturday playing with his foursome, he proposed we play as a family on Sunday, when the course was less busy.

We'd arrive, all pomp and circumstance. Chuck and I had our golf shoes with us and changed in the car; then took our clubs from the trunk and carried them in through the men's locker room, cleats clicking, and up the rubberized ramp into and through the pro shop, out to the crowded first tee. Mom changed in her locker room and Dad in his; then Dad stopped in the pro shop. Irv the caddy master gave him a special greeting (Irv had a withered left arm, and when Chuck or I were there alone, told us how grateful he was to Dad for getting him his job, presumably when Dad had served on the club's board of trustees). Mom got the scorecard and little pencils. Dad asked for his favorite caddy, who could carry double. Irv pulled down their bags from a storage rack in back, and the caddy brought them around to the tee, where Chuck's and my bags were lined up. We all took practice swings with our drivers as groups ahead of us teed off. Then Paul, the florid-faced Irish starter, called out: "Henrys!"

In front of Paul, the caddies, and the players waiting to go after us, each of us stepped up in turn. Dad thwapped the ground with his practice swing, wiped his right hand on his leg, got set, then scoop-swung with a grunt and fell away, sending his drive in the fairway some 200 yards. Mom, next, ten yards forward on the ladies' tee: her back swing twisting high, then swivel and down, topping the ball, so it bounced short of the fairway to the left, at which point she shook her head and waved off Dad's offer of a mulligan. Chuck teed up (and behind us, Paul whispered: "Watch this guy, he's really good!"), took practice swings that clipped the ground with a swish, then squared off at the ball, waggled, then all in one smooth motion hit and followed-through, as his ball carried high down the middle and over the crest. I went last (Paul's whisper: "Kid hits long, but he's wild"), worked my feet into the ground, inhaled, exhaled, checked the fairway, eyes down, concentrated on the ball, started the club head slowly back, pivoted, then swung down hard, hit and followed through, clean, the club and shaft up and behind my neck, and only then looked up to follow my drive straight and low, the equal of Chuck's, or, more likely, a big slice into trees to the right, nearly out of bounds.

Chuck and I would shoulder our bags. The caddy would stop at Mom's ball with Mom, and after she hit a wood into the fairway, and then another, head for Dad's. If I were in the trees, I'd hit out fat and end up way short of the green, or maybe in a sand trap. Dad's four-iron landed short of the green. Chuck's drive was perhaps 80 yards from the hole—a high nine-iron with back spin that rolled back, leaving a twenty-foot putt, which he might miss by five feet, but still make par.

Our games rehearsed our lives. Dad played a game smugly confident in mediocrity. Mom played lamenting the game she used to have. Chuck played well. And I played frustrated and anxious about the game I knew I should have, and did, I thought, on any occasion but this, when I had to prove myself in the eyes of my family.

I took every flubbed shot as a self-betrayal, or as an injustice at the hands of fate; every three-putt green; every out-of-bounds; every choice of too much or too little club. Dad was skeptical, always: "You'll never make that shot." When I did make a clean, pure shot; or when I sank a long putt, he dismissed it as luck, rather than as skill. Mom, meanwhile, over-praised my good shots, bewailed the misses; and never lost her faith in my potential or deserts. As for Chuck, the more miserable I grew, the more he kept aloof. This was only a game. You didn't throw clubs. You didn't break the rules. You didn't spoil it for everyone else. Which isn't to say he didn't get mad at himself, also. The challenge of golf was partly a challenge of temper. By the finishing holes, we played in an ugly, malevolent silence. Dad usually finished in the nineties. Mom never broke one hundred. Chuck broke eighty and I might break ninety, where my personal best, apart from my family, was a 78. Nevertheless, we always looked forward to these games as a family rite.

We also loved the course itself: the manicured five-mile trek of it, the close-cut Bermuda grass of the putting surfaces, the browned, coarser grass of the fairways (cross-hatched from mowing), and the full, thick rough. The whir of cicadas. The lush vistas. The old leafy trees: willows, elms, oaks, and maples. The hills, especially on 13, with the green elevated higher than a house; then from the high tee on 14, the dog-leg left over water and bordered by woods out-of-bounds (often my nemesis, no matter how well I played). The clear, hot pressure of the sun and its dazzle on grass and sand, the watery mirages on humid days. We came to know each hole with its tricks and hazards. I can visualize the course even now, hole by hole, a lifetime later.

Speaking of luck: given Dad's years of regular play, the odds for an occasional miracle were in his favor. At some point, playing with his foursome, he scored an eagle 2 on the long fifth hole, when his three-wood from the fairway trickled onto the green and into the cup. Some years later, towards the end of his life, he made a hole-in-one on 6, thereby joining the club's Hole-in-One Club, which meant he had to stand drinks to the entire lounge, and got an honorary plaque.

*

Dad kept playing until he died at age 72. He and Mom had moved to a single-floor, ranch style "retirement" house in Villanova, with a large enough back yard for us to still practice chip shots when we visited. As for putting, now we had a long carpeted hallway as well as a spacious living room. I kept a bedroom here, as I came back and forth from Massachusetts, first from college, and then from graduate school. Jack and Judy had settled at great distances, Colorado and Virginia. Chuck had married a nurse my age during his four-year residency at nearby Bryn Mawr Hospital; had two boys, and then moved to Winona, New Jersey, to practice as a surgeon at Woodbury Memorial Hospital. When I visited Mom and Dad, we made a new ritual of driving on the freeways over the Walt Whitman bridge to visit him. Before long his third son was born and they moved into a big Victorian in Woodbury. Golf, with its patrician ceremonies, remained central in his life. He joined a country club there and went on golfing junkets with doctor friends to Myrtle Beach and elsewhere. He kept his game up and boasted that he could go professional, if he wanted to; all he needed was time to practice, and the pressure of playing for money.

After my freshman spring at Amherst, when I played briefly with the golf team, golf went out of my life. On visits home, sometimes Chuck visited and we'd either play together at St. Davids, or make a three-some with Dad, with Chuck and me now signed in as guests. I kept my bag, shoes, and clubs with me in my car trunk, but my life was away from home. Writing was my passion. I went from Amherst to years at Harvard in graduate English. I lived at the poverty line, on scholarships, grants, subsidies from Dad, and my first part-time teaching job. On another visit home, before Chuck's sons were old enough to play, he took me as a guest to play his own course. We had this bond.

*

It is the spring of 1976, in Cambridge. Tim O'Brien, a writer friend, who has published two books, and is about to publish a third, and whom I've come to know in connection with the literary magazine I have co-founded, professes a passion for golf, and has his clubs. I tell him that I haven't played for years, but that I used to have a 9 handicap. I keep my clubs with me in the trunk of my car. He invites me to join him and another friend, Sandy, on an expedition to a top-rated public course outside of Boston, Shaker Hills.

Tim is from Minnesota, and from a background similar to mine, but different in being two years younger than I am and having chosen to serve in Vietnam, while I buried myself in graduate school for draft deferments. Sandy is a fellow Vietnam vet and Michael Dukakis's campaign manager. Tim and I are both recently married, but as they pick me up and put my moldy clubs in their car—a convertible, top down—their boisterous talk en route is all about womanizing.

We park and sign in for $20 each. We practice on the putting green, and then I pull out my driver and take big practice swings as we wait, feeling confident despite my years away. The first tee is elevated, with marshy rough below to the left and pines to the right. Both Tim and his friend hit modest drives into the fairway. They step aside and wait for me. My first try, I lift my head as I hit, topping the ball, so it dribbles irretrievably into the marsh. They grant me a mulligan. I settle down, another big swing, and this time the ball pops high and makes it 50 yards or so, just onto the lip of the fairway. We take our bags and set off, stopping at my ball. I take out a three-wood. Practice swing. Aim to the left edge of the fairway, where it bends out of sight. Big swing—and this time not only the ball, but the head of my club flies into the marsh, the club head carrying farther than the ball. I make my red-faced apologies, take the penalty and drop. I hit a decent iron to the bend in the fairway. Including my approach shots, and a four-putt green, my score is 10. Tim has made par 4, his friend a 5. They confer together and agree that they can't take my money. Of course, I had no idea that we are playing for $25 per hole. They decide to go on gambling together, and seeing how pathetic I am, allow me to play along for practice. I'm rusty. It's been a long time. And so it goes. I hit a good shot now and then, a good drive at last, proof of my old game, which is otherwise in ruins. But I am mortified. I am painful to behold, chopping and hacking my way, sometimes even missing the ball. Tim wins over Sandy, one or two holes up. I can imagine their laughter after they drop me off and go for a drink. This is the end of golf for me, I tell Connie back home. I'm humiliated enough by rejections of my novel. I don't need to pay to be humiliated by golf as well. Here too, I realize, I have transferred my rivalry with Chuck, in golf and in life, to Tim, who progresses not only as a professional writer, but who plays in a regular writers' foursome with John Updike.

This same fall, Dad dies unexpectedly.

*

Golf remained central to Chuck's life, along with his surgical practice (and its side benefit of wealth), his family, and his friendships. He tried to initiate each of his three sons over time. Sometime after Dad's death, Connie and our daughter Ruth visited my mother, who now lived alone in the Villanova house, and who had built an enclosed swimming pool that took up the back yard, leaving no more room for our chip shots. Chuck proposed to drive up and join us, and despite my protests that I had lost my game cajoled me into one last round at St. Davids. He brought along his oldest son, 17-year-old Chuck Jr. He paid the green fees himself, as if he were Dad. Since we were no longer members, Irv let us play as his special guests. Against the timelessness of the course, our family rite would pass to a new generation. Chuck Jr., however, showed little aptitude, my own heart had gone out of the game, and even Chuck Sr.'s playing seemed off. The effort felt forced.

I learned later of the tensions in Chuck's parenting. That his marriage had broken up and was headed for divorce. That his boys formed a kind of outlaw band among themselves, and were in and out of trouble with the police; all had drug and alcohol problems; and Chuck Jr. needed therapy for the crippling pressure he felt to live up to Chuck. None finished college.

Soon after his divorce in 1985, our mother died. Chuck served as her executor, overseeing the sale of her house and distribution of inheritance (in our case, allowing us to buy a starter house just in time for the arrival of our adopted son, David, from Korea). Chuck himself moved into a condo, which I visited in 1988. He continued to operate on cancers. He was dating different women, but soon found "the love of his life," Maureen. A divorcee with means, she had her own condo and refused to live with or marry him. Malpractice suits and the high cost of malpractice insurance forced Chuck to retire early, at age 58: embittered and resigned, but determined to enjoy himself. Over the next eight years, he and Maureen traveled abroad; they traveled out West to visit Jack, then Judy, with side visits to his sons in Arizona. In 1995, they went to Kenya, where he performed volunteer surgery, and where they played golf. They visited us. They bought a time-share condo in Los Cobos, Mexico, across from a golf course, and invited us to visit, though we never could or really wanted to. Alone in his New Jersey condo, Chuck often called me long-distance, sounding depressed, especially after one of his long-time golfing buddies died. He spoke of feeling deserted by his sons, who only got in touch when they needed money. A surprise call, this time from Maureen in 1999, brought Connie and me to Woodbury Memorial Hospital and Chuck's bedside a week before his 66th birthday. He was dying of lung cancer, which he had known about over the past year without telling me or anyone else. Maureen was now his wife. They'd been married in a bedside service, cake and all, before she called. She'd called his sons as well, and they now hovered close. Doctor friends stopped by. In the midst all these claims, Chuck sat up and smiled wryly through his pain: "I have more cancer than I have lung," he told me. As memento of their adventures together, Maureen had two albums full of photos, including ones of them putting on a green in Africa. From time to time he stopped listening, concentrating instead on the TV mounted overhead, which was tuned to the golf channel. We left before he died—he did live past his birthday—and by Maureen's account his death was ugly. He was delusional. He wanted to die back in her condo. He strangled at last. But I like to think of him as losing himself in the dream of the players on TV.

*

As I anticipate my own retirement (I am 66 myself now), golf returns to haunt me. Clubs from my boyhood have always drifted through our house, two putters, the nine- and six-irons; the rest are in my cracked and decaying bag out in our storage shed. Now here is my son David, thin and athletic, 22, just graduating from college. Parents wish for their children, not as their children often feel, for themselves (the way I saw my father during the counter-culture Sixties); and before David left home for college, he felt that way about us. "I'm not living to please you! You don't know anything about me!" were the themes of his most frustrated and heart-breaking rages. Except for friends and for sports, he hated school. But then in college he matured. He earned mostly B's, majoring in marketing; he found a long-term, loving girl friend; added fraternity brothers to his life-time friends; traveled and found jobs to support himself; and began to explore his Korean heritage as an adoptee. He has become his own man.

He surprises me with a sudden interest in golf. He's taken my driver, my three-wood, and a three-iron from our shed, and he and Ben—a pal from the pricey prep school where we sacrificed to send him—have visited a driving range in Wellesley. Then Ben's dad had gone out with Ben for nine holes and Dave had gone with them, trying and retrying different shots in practice, using Ben's clubs. Dave wants me to take him.

I welcome this chance for common ground. We gather my clubs and he directs me turn by turn past the Wellesley hospital and off Rt. 16 out to the spacious, well-kept MDC course, where a bucket of balls is $5 and you have your choice of modern, metal-head drivers.

The driving range is behind the club house, and up some stairs: twenty or more tees addressing a low, wide field, with markers from 50 to 250 yards and high net fences to the left and right, shielding the active fairways. A tractor with a scoop and a protected wire-mesh cab crosses back and forth, harvesting the hit balls, and Dave boasts that he and Ben tried to hit it, as if it were a carnival target. The golfers, men, women, varying ages, body types, and skill levels, hit away. We wait until two adjoining tees are free. Dave chops away with a baseball swing, all arms, topping the ball, skying it, or slicing into the net. I help him to adjust his stance and grip, one hand over the other, fingers partly interlocked. I tell him to keep his head down, eye on the ball. In slow motion, facing him, I guide his club: "Keep your head down, think of your left hand leading the swing, push back, imagine a straight line back from the ball, that's it, keep your left arm stiff, don't bend the elbow; lead with your hips first, let your left arm follow, straight, through the ball, and follow through … don't look up, don't push with your right." He tries some practice swings. "Good, but you're still swinging with your arms. Always make your body lead your left arm. Again. And try to close your stance a little." He tees up several more balls, hitting high hooks and slices. Then I step up, and he stops to watch. I take my practice swings; my gut is in my way and I'm stiff as I pivot, but I go through my accustomed motion, thwapping the mat. I tee up a ball and take a long time, concentrating. I want to become the ball. All form: slow back swing, pivot down, and through, resulting in a stubby hook. I try again and this time it goes straight, though not very far. The next few go straight as well, and then I connect and what feels like one of my old-time drives lifts and slices at the 200-yard marker. My best drives here, perhaps every tenth try, go where I aim, but rarely more than 200, and never past 250. "At least they go where you aim, Dad. That's great!" Dave congratulates me. He tries again, and this time, unorthodox form or not, really connects. I am breathless, watching as his drive soars straight, carries past the 250 marker and keeps rolling. "Whoa, that's beautiful, Dave. Terrific hit!" In the carry of his ball, I feel my envy of youth, my pride in him, and my wish for him to thrive, not only in golf, but in all aspects of his life.

Perhaps we can practice together even more. I can recover a semblance of my youth's game. He can learn the different clubs, the irons, the chips, the sand wedge, the putter, the tricks of deliberate hooks and fades, backspin, downhill, uphill, and side-hill lies. Neither of us is ready to play nine holes, but perhaps we can build towards that, reviving all this past.

*

A simple thing, golf. A thing I once did well. A way of life for me, long gone. I am a teacher, an editor, a writer, a husband, a father, in the blue collar suburbs of Boston. I've lived here now most of my life. I've raised my children here. I can't afford a country-club membership, even if I wanted one (I don't); nor do I subscribe to the dream of privilege, caste and measure, which golf suggests. Yet golf is partly who I am, and here the legacy persists: from Thralls to Mom; from Thralls, Mom and Dad to Chuck and to me; from Chuck to me, and to his sons; from me to David, and even to my daughter's daughter, Eva. I feel a sentimental swell in my throat as Eva tries to imitate me and putt on our rug. Age 4, she tries hopelessly with one of my outsized putters; then with her plastic toy set. This seems to come from nowhere.

Perspectives

I know that there is a wholeness to the landscape in which I live. I know this as common sense, as experience, and by documentation and report. I live in Watertown, Mass., ten miles west of Boston, along the Charles River. I teach at Emerson College in downtown Boston, on the Common, and I commute there, mostly by car, along Storrow Drive, following the river the entire way. In warm weather I bike in occasionally. Here, I can show you on a map. Here is my landscape, my world, as seen from above. In fact I have an aerial photograph I tacked to my study's wall; the cover from a 1994 Boston Globe supplement about future planning, the photograph is exactly the same scale as the Boston area street map that I have tacked below it, both showing the Charles River meandering from Watertown, through Cambridge, into the Charles River basin, and then pinched through locks, into Boston harbor. My guess is that this is a view from 30,000 feet, too high to see cars, and higher than I have viewed this landscape while taking off from or circling to land at Logan Airport. The correspondence of photograph to map pleases me. I search for what I know. There among the crusty grid of downtown Boston, crusty because of the shadows cast by high-rise office buildings, is Boston Common. I can't see, but know, 180 Tremont, where I teach, just there, along the Common's lower right margin (for my last two years chairing the Writing Division, my tenth floor office windows overlooked the Common, where flocks of birds, pigeons probably, spread and spiraled, dipped and clustered like my thoughts). And there, the rectilinear serrations of Back Bay, where years earlier from another office twelve floors up, I watched sailboats on the Charles River Basin and was distracted by rock music amplified from the half-shell on the Esplanade. The river loops north at what I know to be the Boston University bridge. Two full hand spans west from Boston Common, that green patch, mossy looking with treetops, is Mt. Auburn Cemetery, then more along the wavy ribbon of river, between what must be the Arsenal Street and North Beacon Street bridges, I see the red roofs of the Arsenal Mall. The river widens, creating an island that marks the local boat club, narrows at Watertown Square, goes north for what I know to be one mile, and there, that bridge marks Bridge Street, two blocks from my house. I think I can make out the square of Bemis playground across from us. My eye hungers, searching for purchase, for connection.

*

I have lived in this landscape for 40 years, ever since graduating from college, one hundred miles west. My first glimpse came as I drove along Route 2 from Amherst for an interview at Harvard that spring. Just over a hill, the city skyline appeared suddenly and clearly in the distance. For years to follow, as I came and went from Harvard, finished my Ph.D. in English in 1971, lived in different Cambridge apartments and neighborhoods, from Harvard Square to Porter Square to Central Square to East Cambridge, before marrying and moving to Watertown, I would get as lost driving outside my neighborhood as if I had just materialized, say, in Atlanta, or Minneapolis, cities utterly unknown to me. Maps were no help. Attempting to return to Cambridge from a dance club or party in downtown Boston, I would end up somehow on the north shore, Chelsea, say, or Revere. I learned the city by getting lost. North, South, West. Shortly after I met Connie, who would become my wife, she got an emergency call at my Central Square apartment telling her that her father had just died in Florida; her married sister, Lonne, lived in Waltham, across from Brandeis, and would I drive her there? I had never driven out Mt.

Auburn Street from Harvard Square, but with Connie choked and distraught beside me, and somehow reading directions from a paper in her lap, we headed past Mt. Auburn Hospital, then Mt. Auburn Cemetery, a dingy, over-traveled route with bus wires overhead and unused trolley tracks. I had no idea where I was going, or how much farther, but on the way I did count some seventeen funeral homes, each one a jolt in our faces, given Connie's grief, each for some other denomination or ethnicity, Armenian, Greek, Italian, Irish (given the names, O'Reilly, say, or Adrossinian). The drive seemed surreal, a pilgrimage of grief into unknown destinations. Eventually we reached an apartment complex across from Brandeis University, where all at once I met most of this girl's family, sister, brother-in-law, niece, brother, brother-in-law's local parents and sisters, a sudden blur of intimacy and tribal embrace. Two years later, having lived together in two different Cambridge apartments, we were married at Connie's mother's home in Miami, Florida, surrounded by both our families; then with the idea of starting our own family, we found an inexpensive apartment out that same Mt. Auburn Street route, in Watertown. In contrast to the sordid singles world of Cambridge, Watertown seemed populated by working-class, first- and second-generation ethnic families. Shrines in front yards. Grape arbors. Laundry flapping in backyards, neighbors watching out for neighbors, village-style vegetable gardens. Our apartment was on the first floor of a two family frame house, owned by Italian immigrants, who shouted "Mange! Mange!" through our ceiling, and who were cursed in English by their assimilated children. Mt. Auburn Street became my daily commute. The literary magazine *Ploughshares,* which I had co-founded while I lived in Central Square, had already become my life, and its post office box in Central Square had to be emptied daily. I was teaching part-time now at Emerson, at Harvard, at Simmons, at Northeastern. My own father died in Philadelphia, just after we moved. Connie was pregnant. My widowed mother came to visit. Our daughter Ruth was born. Connie's water had broken, contractions begun, and I drove as fast and carefully as I could through traffic to the hospital near Simmons College, having practiced the route for just this occasion.

Two days after the birth, I drove Connie and the baby home. Twenty-one years later to the day, my daughter has her first apartment across the grid of Boston, off Huntington Avenue, and after I find my way there to loan her our car for the birthday weekend, she is driving me back to Watertown, turning down Longwood to the Fenway, when I realize that we are retracing her first trip home.

*

I had begun my fifties believing in my "self"—even after the setbacks of infertility in my marriage (which had been resolved by adoption of my son as an infant from Korea)—and the rejection of my work as a writer. I had lost my father when I was thirty-five, my mother when I was forty-four. My two older brothers and older sister were scattered and distant: New Jersey, Colorado, Los Angeles. My closest friend, literary and personal, Richard Yates, died when I was fifty-one. I still believed that I was meant for recognition as a writer. I loved my family. I had built up *Ploughshares,* seeking to redress what I saw as the discouragement of literature in the marketplace, and had done so, lacking money, by relying on friendships, talent, resourcefulness and zeal. In the heyday of the National Endowment of the Arts, one muckraking malcontent had even called me "the old grants baron." Beginning in 1984, I had found my first full-time job teaching at Emerson College. With some frustrations, things there had gone well, and I got tenure in 1989, became chair of the writing division, and negotiated the college's acquisition of *Ploughshares.* I felt that as chair I had accomplished miracles in hiring, in curriculum, and in enrollments, to everybody's benefit. If there were soreheads in my fold, I had them well outnumbered in votes and in support from students and the administration, as well as in the world at large. But then a series of circumstances combined. The professor who had originally hired me, who had then stepped down as chair, elected to retire. My campus rival, an older man whose tenure I opposed in my chairperson role, was diagnosed with cancer, won sympathy across campus, was given tenure, and while active in the faculty union, wrote a new contract tailored to his personal situation and calling for faculty evaluation of chairs. Governance at the top of the college had gone berserk. An autocratic president was driven out; and after open war between the college trustees and the faculty, an insider faculty member had become president and needed the support of the faculty union. At this point, 5–4, my faculty voted against my renewal as chair, apparently inflamed by my rival. I couldn't believe that my friends, especially those that I had hired and supported for tenure, could turn on me, as coldly as strangers. I couldn't believe that I had so misread the terrain of interests and power in which I was located. I still can't, these long years later.

Once I was demoted, and one of these friends was put in as acting chair, I was also forced to surrender any real role in *Ploughshares* as my protégé took full control. As for my writing life, I had the support of an agent and had published a selection of best stories from *Ploughshares,* but my novel, which I had rewritten for a third time, along with a new second book, my family's biography, were rejected repeatedly, until the agent gave up.

*

Here is my driver's license description: age 58, male, white, 5 feet 10 inches height, 167 pounds weight, eyes green (glasses required), hair brown, thinning and graying. My fingerprints are on file, my dental records. Here is biology's map. Here is medicine's. Here are the microscopic reports of my infertility, say (16 million sperm per cc, 30 percent motility, 40 percent forward progression). Some day there may be the surprise of other microscopic reports of some part gone wrong, bringing closer the sentence of an ending. Not may be, will be. I know that.

In the spirit of Walt Whitman, I can sing my body electric, cataloguing its thoroughfares and provinces. Not biology's map, but imagination's, totemized fact. My eyes tour and swivel like cameras; some parts impossible to see, or rarely seen, craning in mirrors.

Eyes closed, felt: the rise of each breath, lungs full, the nostril sting of breathing in; then diaphragm and chest muscles contracting, exhale, again, again. Heart's pump.

I shower, I wash the body. I groom the body, shave, regarding in the mirror the reassurance of reflection. How I look. My outside appearance. I touch my neck, my image shows the touch, but I feel the touch also. I close my eyes. I feel the touch.

The body hungers. Weakens, hungers. Desires. Aches. Sleeps, rises. Is ill, in pain. Is well. Floods with pleasure; pleases others. I take it for granted.

I dress the body.

I see myself in still photography, in movies, instant, recent, long ago. I see myself in live video, there, on that TV, where I am used to seeing news and movies.

*

The oldest question of all: if you're not here, here in my daily life, proximate in Boston MA 1998, do you exist? You, reader, whom I have never met? You, my daughter, out of touch, first at Hampshire College, now in Guatemala on field study? You, my mother, dead since 1983? You, my father, dead since 1976? You, Richard Yates, dead since 1992? You, my sister Judy, in Pasadena; my oldest brother Jack in Colorado; my older brother Charles in New Jersey and now and then on a cruise on the *Queen Mary II*? My mother-in-law, Hazel, in Manhattan? My friend Jim McPherson in Iowa City? All structures of connectedness seem ephemeral, even my son today at school, my wife at school. What faith, what knowing or certainty can close these distances?

My mother in the last years, living alone in Philadelphia, used to say when we visited, "that the years fell away." We phone across space, speak our words in real time, with familiar voices. We write letters, we electronically mail thoughts and news in words. We send pictures. Very soon we will all have some form of videophones and can watch each other and speak in real time no matter how distant on or off of this planet. We send audio, video for the keeping. Take family videos; capture family moments.

We are perhaps artists. We remember and imagine each other in episodes, in images, in memory loops. We embody our meaning—

our disembodied selves—in art, in painting, music, stories. I teach Jim McPherson's stories and he comes all alive for me. I teach Richard Yates and, as Tim O'Brien has written (in "Lives of the Dead"), being dead is "like being inside a book that nobody's reading"; as I read, Yates is all alive, his humor, his precision, his generous heart.

I think of, when I was a teenager, my sister's empty room and those upstairs of my departed brothers, after each had left home for independent, adult lives. I would linger in their spaces, surrounded by their possessions and auras.

I live as if things don't matter, as if I don't feel, as if I don't long for lives lost and beyond interaction; but on the other side of numbness, I fear my howl of abandonment, my animal cry to emptiness.

*

"DPs" they were called. "Displaced Persons." I was ten or eleven in those years between the end of World War II and the beginning of the Korean Conflict. They were Eastern European refugees walking in oddly misfitting and somehow foreign clothes and shoes along the back streets of Wayne and St. Davids, streets flanked by the houses and acres of suburban privilege. There must have been some charity relief organization that had found host families in our neighborhood to employ such refugees as maids, butlers, groundspeople. Or perhaps the Valley Forge Military Academy, two miles away from my house down those back roads, was where they worked. I know the sight of them troubled me, their sense of being lost where I was found. A "DP" named Manfred had appeared in my sixth grade class at Radnor Public School, circa 1952. When our town fire siren sounded each noon, our local custom, he scrambled to dive under a desk, because Manfred had been in real bombing raids. Also, he was obsessed with washing his hands in our deep arts sink in the back of the classroom, relishing the bar of Ivory soap as a luxury. Most of us, most of the class, rejected and mocked him as peculiar, except for the fattest girl in the class, who took him over as her special project.

Some years later, as Castro took over Cuba, Cuban refugees began appearing. I remember my father hiring several in our family candy factory for menial labor and remarking that one of them had been a surgeon, but couldn't practice in America.

*

E. M. Forster writes: "We cannot understand each other, except in a rough-and-ready way; we cannot reveal ourselves, even when we want to; what we call intimacy is only a makeshift; perfect knowledge is an illusion. [Fictional people] are people whose secret lives are visible or might be visible; we are people whose secret lives are invisible."

There are no secrets in art, because we agree that art is an act of imagination, an as if, rather than a literal experience with literal consequences. You paint your deepest emotions. I write myself to a place of open mystery. In real life, however, daily life—the life of compacts, trusts, reliabilities—stark frankness is wounding and offensive, denies necessary fictions (such as fatherhood, husband-hood, friendship, teacher-hood, citizenship, team person-ship), and in denying becomes itself a lie, a withholding.

This may be the basis of Catholic confession, and of prayer in general. If there is a God who knows everything, whose understanding is infinite and forgiving, then we are not alone. We believe in divine intimacy. We make or dream a space of utter vulnerability, beyond self-deceptions and working truths.

*

Abused, forgetting becomes a power of pathology, a denial of life, a repression in psychological terms. I push myself away, estranged. Used correctly, I suppose, forgetting is "forget and forgive," though without remembering how do you forgive, and without forgiving, how do you forget?

*

I have believed too readily that life is a quest for some absolute perspective, some final clarification. That adulthood itself is always that next horizon, that higher and wider perspective, from which everything becomes clear. That all experience, human experience, my experience, will overlap and coincide and I will be with the old men on Yeats's lapis lazuli, looking down on the spectacle of human folly and ignorance and futures, and my glittering eyes will be gay.

I think of the perspectives of Zen. The idea of reincarnation, of one life-stage progressing in perspective to the next until one reaches Nirvana. I think of the "epiphany" in fiction as speaking for our faith in endings; of John Keats and his 24-year-old vision of "stepping towards truth."

But I don't know.

At the end, we see perhaps what we wished we saw, just as we do each night in dreams. Perhaps the quest for perspective is life's makework. We search, we study, we dream. In small ways we acquire small wisdoms. And yet we forget more than we remember. In my own life how often I have willingly walked by hints and clues, and even by life's angels. I have chosen not to ask. Not to see. Not to know.

And then it comes. Your ending. It happens. Swiftly as fact. This is happening. Or slowly, and in pain, nine months, nine weeks. Your body claims your mind. Your body and your mind are one. Failing. Too tired to think, too weak.

Yes.

No.

Rosebud.

Deaths in My Life

My first felt death was that of my father, when he was 70 and I was 35. His death occurred at a physical and emotional distance from my adult life, without real warning, and no real goodbye, other than the cumulative goodbyes, in health, of glad escapes from his closed horizons in suburban Philadelphia—the world of his own father, his boyhood, and his working and family life—and returns to my life in Boston, college, graduate school, and finally marriage and a teaching job. One day my mother called, with a strained, shaken voice, and told me he had gone into the hospital (where I had only seen him once, years before, after he had had a gall bladder attack, and he had laughed at my saucer eyes, as if I were seeing him on his deathbed). He had jaundice. My older brother, Chuck, a surgeon in nearby New Jersey, was stopping up every day to look in on him. No need to be alarmed, no need to visit. You have your busy life, your teaching. He will be fine. And then she called again, he had to have an operation. And then, again, my oldest brother Jack was visiting from Colorado; and then Jack had gotten on the phone to say hello, and Dad was fine, he'd seen him and he was sallow-skinned, but in good spirits. Jack returned to Colorado. Another call: Dad had come through the operation on his liver, but was in a coma. No, don't come down. She was at his side, wanted to be there when he woke up. Some trouble now with his kidneys. The doctors said he was unconscious and couldn't feel pain, but he was crying out so loudly the other patients were saying can't they give that man something? And then the call: he'd died. Urine had gotten into his bloodstream and poisoned his brain. All within a week or ten days from the first call.

My wife Connie and I drove down for the funeral. There was no viewing. My mother said we wouldn't want to see him, the way his body was at the end. We filled their house— their retirement house—in Villanova, Judy from Arizona, Jack from Colorado, Chuck from New Jersey, along with our spouses. My mother wanted only us, our nuclear family, not my aunts on my father's side. A limousine picked us up, a silent, stoic company, confused in loss as we had been in life between love and guilt, each of us somehow having wished him out of our lives, and out of our mother's. She had chosen the most expensive coffin and arranged for a graveside service with the Presbyterian minister because "he would have wanted it that way." No tears, at least on the outside. What I recall is silence and inexorability.

The grave was in a family plot, purchased originally by my father's father in West Laurel Hill, a fashionable Main Line cemetery. We had been dragged here repeatedly as children and teenagers to put Easter flowers on my grandfather's broad stone at the head of the plot, which was engraved with my name (against my mother's wishes, as the last of four children, I had been named after him); he had died in 1948, when I was seven; then in 1969 my grandmother had joined him, having spent her last years in a posh nursing home; and most recently my uncle John Spaeth, a spouse, had been buried in 1974. The plot was laid out with spaces reserved for descendants, first the head grave, then those for each of three children and their spouses, my father and his two younger sisters; then under those plots, graves for their children and their children's spouses..

What ritual there was felt foreign and offensive, a mockery, words by the minister about the Kingdom of Heaven, about Dad as a loving husband and father, and then the coffin slowly cranked down. I remember, for all my irony, my disbelief, amounting almost to panic, that my father, so vivid to me always, was somehow in that casket.

Alive, loved, troublesome, powerful; and that was him in there and being lowered into the earth. I couldn't believe that that was him even though I knew it was.

I remember our returning home and eating, eating, eating ravenously. Halloween was only a day or so away, and perhaps our most genuine gesture, as bizarre and true as we felt we were, was while on some errand, on impulse to go into the local toy store, Halligan's—a mecca at least of my own childhood—and buy clear plastic masks, the kind that eerily distort your features into Nixon's, say. We wore them driving back to Villanova; and laughed and laughed together as we tried on different faces for each other, my mother too.

*

Eight years later we gathered again at West Laurel Hill for my mother's funeral, in September 9, 1985. I was 44 and my daughter Ruth, conceived just months after my father's death, was 7.

My mother had lived a widow's life, alone all this time in the Villanova house. She had visited us two or three times in our Boston apartment after Ruth was born; then later we visited her with Ruth for several Christmases. "I know you know what loneliness is," she said to me once. She hadn't the energy to move or travel and make new friends. She did attend a Cornell class reunion and discover several classmates, with whom she corresponded.

We had nine months warning, from her diagnosis with degenerative heart failure. The first episode had been on February 27. There had been a surprise midnight call from Chuck telling us she was okay—had gone into intensive care in the cardiac unit at Bryn Mawr Hospital. She, when we spoke to her, said she had thought she had gone over, but she wasn't good enough. They'd thrown her back, like an undersized fish.

Connie and Ruth stayed with her for some nine weeks, while I came and went back to Boston and my job. My sister came and left. Jack came and left. Chuck came up from New Jersey as often as he could. But there were stretches, too, covered only by a live-in nurse (who smoked and otherwise got on Mom's nerves). We were there with Chuck, when he showed her her cardiologist's letter. She read the letter, then asked Chuck directly:

"How long do I have? Three months? Three years?"

He looked at her steadily: "Yes."

"Which?"

"Yes," he repeated.

Over spring and summer, we lived her decline and closure. As the disease progressed, as there were other episodes of hospitalization, a portable bottle of oxygen became a fixture, to be refilled from full-sized tanks as tall as she was, which were delivered by a medical service (all on Medicaid) and which stood like sentinels in a corner by her bed. She lived now in oxygen, with plastic nose clips.

She woke one morning I was there, feeling, she said, "like a girl, ready to get up and chase and spank babies...."

One of the last last times (there were five or six), I drove back to Boston on the New York parkways, 2 in the morning, filled with the sense of losing her. I had the overpowering sense of her spiritual presence, that at this moment, this, as I drove, she had died; and feeling that so utterly, this was my time of weeping and farewell.

Chuck called at 5 a.m., first dawn, September 6, 1985, and said that she was gone.

She had asked to be cremated, a first in our family. Again we gathered at the West Laurel Hill plot. Judy and her husband Hans, and the grandchildren, John, Lucia, Bonnie; Jack and his wife June and the granddaughter Terry; Chuck and his wife Nancy, and sons, Chucky, Bob and Scott; Connie, Ruth and I. Her Sister Janice and Uncle Lloyd from New Hampshire. We each laid a yellow rose on the casket, which held the urn. Again the minister, a stranger to us; and again the graveside service: words so empty that they seemed like an offense.

She was Ruth's first death.

David Jung Min Henry, my adopted son, only an idea or hope at the time, which we had talked about with Mom, would be born some twelve thousand miles away in Korea one week later, September 15.

*

More deaths followed in my life, in Connie's, and in our children's. I think of a painting by my nephew, John Friedericy, Judy's oldest son, before Mom died. There are in four rows, some sixteen heads, "the people in my life," he called it. His mother, his father, my mother, my father, his two sisters, his lover Bruce, one of his older teachers, other best friends. Most of the faces look out at the viewer. But three, eyes closed and ashen, face left: they were the dead in his life at the time of his painting, including my father. John himself died of AIDS at age 35, in 1990, after two years of treatment and decline. My sister and Hans had divorced shortly after Mom's death, and purportedly Hans had not condoned John's homosexual lifestyle. I saw John on my first visit ever to San Francisco, for a writers' convention, before he knew he had AIDS. Later, after he was ill, and visiting Judy in Los Angeles, their home place for years, Connie flew out with David and Ruth to see him. Typically in one snapshot from that visit, John, mustached and balding, poses in my sister's backyard with a suction-tipped arrow dangling from his forehead, hamming the pose of either El Greco's crucifixion or the Temptation of St. Anthony or both, flanked by his mother in blue sunglasses and his partner Bruce, Connie, and my children on the other side. He would in the two years to come be hospitalized repeatedly with pneumonia and be surrounded by his sisters, his mother, and his friends, as he grew weaker.

I did send him a goodbye letter, near the end, but before he was ready to accept it. I wrote him that I was grateful he and I had our visit in San Francisco, "to catch up and re-relate and to be family and friends. I don't know how to say goodbye, or quite how to be normal under the shadow of goodbye, though I have lived it once, with your grandmother.... In your grammy's case, I felt she'd given me *me,* that I had her love to live up to. In yours, at this distance, you've given us your work, which is what you have been given to give, and says you. Your exuberance is there, your relish of life, your wit, as well as your puzzlement, anger, pain and steady strength.... Our gain is having known you, and continuing to love and feel that essence that is you; our loss is missing you and missing your continued growing and experience and all that you would have given still, but have not been given to give.... In missing, or in getting ready to miss you, what I feel, John, is a debt."

He wrote back, thanking me for the letter, explaining that his doctor thought by the time John's tolerance for AZT wore off, that "there will surely be a new legalized treatment for me.... This combined with my strength makes me confident that I can stay ahead of the game.... They hope that AIDS will become something to be lived with, not cured, rather like diabetes." He was confident that "there are years (and maybe decades) left." Meanwhile he had his drawing, painting, and sculpture: "I don't think people die until their life's purpose is taken away from them—and I'm not ready to retire yet." He also described a collaboration with his oldest sister, Lucia, making collector dolls. "The dolls are one of a kind, made of porcelain and covered in beeswax. I sculpt the hands, feet and heads, hollow and fire them, and the Lucia paints faces, dips them in beeswax and creates the characters."

*

Four years after John died, I flew to Los Angeles to see Judy for the third time since our mother's funeral. She was 59; I was just turning 53. I knew from phone conversations that she had continued in John's place to collaborate with Lucia and that Friedericy Dolls was now an established, thriving business. Also that she had dedicated herself for the past two years as a volunteer in a "buddy" relationship with a young girl, Jessica, who had been born with AIDS, and who would die before much longer. She wouldn't be in her Pasadena cottage to greet me when I arrived, but told me the key would be in the mailbox. How strange to enter her intimate world, the shell of her living with the opening of that door.

Paintings filled nearly every available portion of wall, foyer, living room, dining room, bedroom. Mostly the paintings were John's, some original canvases I had seen in his San Francisco apartment, some I had only seen in slides, and now was startled by in full size and richness of color. Other paintings I recognized as my mother's and Judy's. John's sculptures, too, occupied every available surface. Nudes, primarily female, were everywhere. Paper mache stylized birds of John's hung on wires from the ceiling. Startling dolls peered from tables, corners, chairs, in size ranging from twelve inches high to some thirty-six (a Don Quixote seated on a horse, Quixote's face resembling my brother Jack's, stood before the fireplace). As I waited for Judy, I told her later, I didn't feel alone. The house and its art told her silence over time, and told John's. The walls talked, the corners, every table, every square and cubic inch. John's art merged with my mother's, with Judy's, and with the dolls and sculptures that were Judy's and Lucia's. I felt as if death were no more than a continuum of absence in space and in time, like physical distances between the living.

Judy had a meeting of her "buddies" hospice group the next night and took me along. After John's death, his lover Bruce, who had infected him, attempted suicide by jumping off a roof, only to end up maimed. Judy had taken care of Bruce until his own death from AIDS. It seemed to me that out of her love for John, her mission was to immerse herself in the problems of the gay community, especially the AIDS community. Not to flinch, as Hans had done, and turn away; but to immerse herself. And in the Buddies meeting this night, she tried to comfort another Buddy, a librarian, who had just been told by the social worker in front of us that her buddy/girl had taken a turn for the worse, and that the doctor had told her, the social worker, in medical confidence, that the girl would not recover and would die soon. The librarian had broken down in tears.

A spare bedroom was cluttered with archives of John's work as well some incomplete mosaics and canvasses of her own. Within the creation of the house and its shown art, there was the so-called studio, where an archive of all John's sketches, notebooks, letters, and other papers were stored in flat art drawers. Also where unhung canvases of his leaned against one wall, and where the entire original of a series of lithographs called *Heron Dance* was leaning on an easel ("I put up a new panel each week"). There were two mosaics messily in progress and abandoned on cluttered worktables. Of her own painting and sketching the canvas propped on one of those tables that gripped me was indeed a self-portrait. "I did that after John died," she said. It was stark, all brown and white, a face contemplating suicide. Angry, empty, devastated, blank. The stunned, helpless, beyond howls and tears face of a Hiroshima survivor, or victim waiting for execution.

There was a nine- or twelve-inch doll on her dresser, in front of her mirror (a mirror stuffed with snapshots of family and friends and her buddy Jessica) that I took for another self-portrait, though she said it was not. This was a life-worn woman lifted young and shining, if those are the words, arched somehow, all alive, enthralled, as if in exaltation, out of her aging body and mortality, as if to greet the lost love found, the dead reborn.

I felt proud of my sister, who seemed to know more about the mysteries of grief than anyone in my life; and who, for me, embodied the triumph of love.

Embodiment

"All comfortable? Let your arms hang down, that's it." She pulled a stool around and sat in front of my head. She was perhaps thirty-three years old, with blond, shoulder-length hair and a chunky build, dressed in slacks, a pullover and a vest. She'd introduced herself as Doreen, and then had left me, telling me to undress, to take off or keep on my underpants, however I felt most comfortable (I kept them on), and then to lie down on my stomach on the massage table, with the sheet pulled up. When I was ready, she'd knocked and come back in.

"Now tell me a little about you. You've never had a massage before?"

"No, never. The people I work with gave me this for Christmas. I've only known massage as a decadent, self-indulgent, privilege-class thing, like Elizabeth Taylor in the movies, mud-masked and naked on her back, with some lifeguard type rubbing oil in."

"That's what most people think," she said. "That or the massage-parlor thing." Her tone seemed to dissociate the professional massage from either.

"I'm a runner. I train for marathons. I've always eyed the massage tables at races. This morning, with the thaw, is the first I've gotten out for a real run in weeks and I'm a little sore. You know, with all this snow, I've been stuck on a stationary bike in my basement."

"Are you married?"

"Yes," I answered, "but we haven't been romantic recently."

"I know. There's a lot of that."

"We're friends. We're compassionate. We have two children, a daughter sixteen, son eight. I'm fifty-two."

"Okay, let's get started." She stood and lifted off my glasses. "Let me take those. Just stay relaxed, arms down, just totally limp. That's good. Don't fight it." Then she moved around and stood alongside my hips, pressing her body close, establishing contact.

"I need to be touched," I went on, in the vein of telling about myself. "I'm not touched a lot in my life, I feel. I am a tense, interior person. I think if we all touched and were touched more, we would be kinder, healthier people.... Normally I take my tension out in running ... and in writing ... I am a writer."

"Well, it's catching on more," she said. "A lot of people are looking to massage for better health; it has health benefits, not just for aches and pains, or muscular or chiropractorish conditions, but for the whole person."

The Indian raga music wove sinuously in the background, atonal and repetitive.

"You have a nice body," she said, working on my back, shoulders and neck. "You take care of yourself."

"Well, like I said, I am a runner."

"I am going to go deep, now, so tell me if it hurts, okay?"

"I have a friend," I said. "A poet, Frank Bidart. He wrote this long poem called 'The War of Vladimir Nijinsky,' about this ballet star Nijinsky who, when he danced, danced World War I, moved to emotions of the war, expressed the war through his body. I feel that way about running. That I am driven to run the 1980s and 1990s in America as I have felt them; that I am saying and feeling what I have lived through the rhythm and grace and endurance of my body."

She shifted to work on my lower body then, kneading the sole of my foot and toes, bending my leg slowly back, farther, until it hurt, stretching; then the other foot.

"I feel like you're talking to me," I said. "You are telling me things. We are having a conversation somehow."

"We are," she said. "Giving a massage for me is like running is for you, the way you described it."

I hadn't asked and didn't ask outright about her life, though I wondered. Was she married? Did she have children? Were her parents alive? Was she lonely? Did she have a lover? I felt that she was telling me as a stranger the weight and meaning of her life, her passages, her experience, her pleasures even.

Several times during the session the sitar tape ran out, and she stopped for a moment to turn it over or to put in a new one. But the twangy, twining strains continued and provided the rhythmic background for her touch.

"I'm not in very good shape," she said. "I couldn't run across the street if you paid me. My arms and shoulders are strong from doing this, but my belly and the rest of me is all soft."

As she bent, working over my buttocks and lower back, I felt or thought I felt her breasts brushing me.

"Time to turn over," she said.

I worried about having an erection, as if that would be disrespectful, and managed not to, as she discretely folded the sheet up, exposing my waist and crotch, then rolled up the rim of my red jockey briefs so that she could oil and massage the flow of my leg muscles deep into the pelvic joints.

Up my legs. Deep into my stomach, up my ribs, over my chest. I turned over on my stomach again and she rubbed warm body oil, lightly scented, into my back and shoulders, then down my legs and leg muscles, all the way to my feet. Then when she finished, she wiped the same areas clean with the warm, damp towel.

We had become speechless, or I had, as we sank together into the rhythm and pleasure. A part of me felt the lover's surge to meet her touch and go forward to real sex, but I was still. I was being done to, with a prohibition against doing. I surrendered, and the rhythm built deeper and deeper towards some primitive center in me, so that I was thinking, and allowed myself to think, of being mothered and swaddled like an infant, so that I was thinking of my mother, and loving and missing her, and weeping at that deep-body memory, my grief inseparable from love, unspeakable love, being tendered, being loved: this was what I wanted and missed most in my life.

She worked on my sacroiliac, where backbone joined pelvis, where my arthritis had been in my earlier thirties, where all the anger and frustration of my loneliness through my single, student years in Cambridge had found its physical outcry, and where later my frustrations as a writer had settled, my years of joblessness once I had my PhD, my fear of marriage, and then of the added compromise of children, and the conflict with my wife who had married me expressly to have children. Thumbs first, pressing, circling into the pelvic joint, heels of both hands, her whole weight leaned. Force, then tenderness; the contact deepening. I groaned.

The birth of our daughter, our infertility ordeal, and our last resort: counseling. "We don't share!" my wife shouted at me. "We don't want the same things. You don't want to adopt because the child won't be smart enough. I'm for life, I'm not 'desperate,' I'm tired of it! You won't talk to me! You need a third person to talk to!" Grief for my father's, and then my mother's death. Grief for dreams denied, for the rejection of my best work as a writer. Grief for betrayals, for my life's first enemies and rivals. Political attempts at Emerson to deny me tenure and to exploit the Writing Department as I had developed it. My friend of twelve years and co-founder of the literary magazine that I had convinced Emerson to sponsor, suddenly claiming credit for my work, then trying to sell the magazine to another university without me for his personal gain. Prolonged legal struggles, as bitter as divorce. Grief for my older sister's grief, first for her husband's departure after thirty years, second for the loss of her son, a promising artist, to AIDS. Grief for the recent death of the novelist Richard Yates, my best friend and mentor, at the age of sixty-six. Six months later, then, death of my arch-rival at Emerson, a popular teacher whose tenure I had opposed just as the man learned he had cancer; the teacher then had rallied sympathy on campus, had gotten tenure, and proceeded to undermine my authority as chair. The turning, inspired by this man before his death, of factions in my faculty against me. My vertiginous mid-life identity, as again, others disdained my meaning and my life's giving. My bid again to publish a book, my masterpiece, without success. And meanwhile, at home, lack of support. My wife's investing her time and heart in her work and friends at the private K-through-six school, where for the past ten years she had established a career as a gifted teacher. My daughter's pulling away into an independent social life. My son's absence as he increasingly played with the children of my wife's friends. My first experiences of impotence—a new, depressing event for me. Memories of my daughter's birth, my son's arrival as an infant. Grief for my sterility and aging as I watched a Nova special on *The Miracle of Birth*. Wonder at the mystery of all that viscera-turned-spirit. Wanting to give life, make life. Wanting to send seeds of personality and value, salmon-like, into the uterus of a resistant world—to send them alive and capable of igniting life in some karmic egg, random and appropriate and waiting.

She found things in me, in my muscles and body, that I hadn't said and maybe couldn't say otherwise.

I was being hot-oiled. I was being caressed.

I was weeping. Then at deep, deep peace.

She had worked her way now back to my shoulders and arms, and up the nape of my neck, and let her fingers trail fondly through my hair. The tape had finished. Silence. My eyes were closed.

"It was a pleasure meeting you," she said. "I'm going now. You can stay here as long as you like. Don't get up all at once, just hold onto it as long as you can."

"Thank you. You're quite, quite wonderful."

Then she had slipped out.

Ten or fifteen minutes later, I did get up and dress, holding the quiet inside myself, the gladness, and after the final business of tying my sneakers and pulling on my coat, I left a five-dollar tip in the dish marked for that purpose (feeling that I could afford to be generous) and left the room. As I stepped through the waiting room, I looked for her. (What had her name been? Doreen?) Where had she gone? There were several young women talking, and the girl at the desk, but no sign of her. Maybe she had had another client, pronto; maybe after a one-hour session, she was free to go home or to take a break. After that much shared emotional experience, she must be shaken too. I didn't ask. I just let myself out into the overcast, darkling late afternoon, and started back to my car. Part of the masseuse's professional technique, I assumed, was in fact to disappear, so that there would not be out-of-session contact.

I had forgotten exactly what she looked like, and was doubtful I could recognize her, especially in street clothes, but I had some notion we might pass if she were heading home too, and maybe we could have coffee. I felt attractive and aglow with beneficent well-being. Then as I turned the corner, a woman who was bundled up and stepping out a back door, and who might have been her or might simply have been a stranger, smiled and looked me in the face. "It's starting again already!" she said. And only a few uncertain steps past her, feeling at first that she meant the world itself, real time itself, I realized that instead she must have meant the snow, scattered flakes falling, followed by the heavier, driving onset. I realized that she had only been a stranger passing, responding to my open glow and commenting on the weather, which was our natural lot.

Looking through the Knothole

In 1939, my father returned home to Philadelphia from a career with the Walter Baker Company in Boston (at the time a division of General Foods), because my grandfather had had a heart attack and our family's chocolate factory was at risk. Having sacrificed a bright future, he soon grew embittered by the business, by my grandfather's oversight, and by the hardships of the war, all of which put a strain on his own marriage and parenting, and led to his alcoholic collapse. Later, given the crisis that the candy company had brought to all of our lives, he vowed never to burden any of us, his own children, with such a life.

To his credit, he never did. I am now a college teacher, a writer, an editor, and have made my life in Boston. Our candy factory has long since been sold. The houses we once lived in have been sold and resold, and the largest, on Bloomingdale Avenue in Wayne, has been turned into condos. My parents are both buried in the family plot that my grandfather purchased in West Laurel Hill Cemetery. With his own table-sized stone at the head, engraved with my name, his vision was dynastic: my grandmother, with a marker just below his, then their three children and spouses, and then room for their children's children and perhaps even more.

When I revisited Wayne in 1985, the summer of my mother's dying, my wife, daughter and I drove those familiar streets and I groped for recognitions and for landmarks to point out. Everywhere the streets seemed narrower and blocks shorter than in memory: the old high school, now the middle school; my old primary school an administration building. The familiar names of tradesmen in the business district were gone, although the buildings remained: Moffo's Shoe Repair (the shoemaker's daughter, Anna, had become an opera star), The Men and Boys Shop, Harrison's, Espenshades, Woolworth's, Brooks' Stationery, Wack's Druggists. The Anthony Wayne movie theater was still there, the Presbyterian Church, the firehouse, the Wayne Title and Trust Clock, although the bank itself had moved. New to Wayne, recognizable franchises adjoined the supermarket: Starbucks, Wendy's, Borders. The mile along the Lancaster Pike between Wayne and St. Davids was now an unbroken strip of malls, indistinguishable from those in anywhere, USA.

Our St. Davids house looked much the same, though somehow in better repair. On an impulse, we stopped in, and were greeted at the back door by a man younger than me, the new owner. A lawyer, I think; perhaps a stockbroker. I explained that I had lived there once, and graciously, he had invited us in. He said something about their having remodeled the kitchen, and when carpenters had torn up the floor, they had said that there must have been a lot of living there, that they sensed spirits. Walls had been knocked down. A modern cooking island. His wife and children were out, and he offered to show us all through the house, but we shyly declined. He had never heard of us by name.

The area is humid and lush in vegetation in summers. Old trees interlock over the roads, creating dappled canopies. Cicadas chirr. I dated girls from many of these houses. I graduated from public school. I loved the woods and fields of outlying farms (such as those in Chadds Ford, painted by Andrew Wyeth) and the nearby Valley Forge State Park. The year before my daughter was born, we had gathered for my father's funeral; and now again, eight years later, we were all back trading visits to care for my mother—Connie, Ruth and I from Boston; Chuck, from his surgeon's life in New Jersey; Jack, from his working-class life in Colorado; Judy from her husband and three children in Arizona. We all had our memories. When my car broke down and was towed away for junk, my mother gave me her boat-sized Buick LaSabre, with air-conditioning; inhabiting her lifestyle as we shopped for groceries, I felt self-conscious in the masquerade. She even paid for Ruth to attend a horse-riding camp and we have the picture: Ruth dressed up in riding gear, helmet, crop and all, sitting on her horse.

*

For three generations the Henrys had prided themselves on being one of the founding families of Wayne. There was my great-grandfather John, who had emigrated from Ireland to Philadelphia at the age of fifteen; by age twenty-six, he had established a milk route in the city, married, lost his first son and wife, and remarried; and by age thirty-six, in 1871, he bought a hundred-acre dairy farm and became the town's milkman. He also helped to found and build the Wayne Presbyterian Church, where he served as Deacon; and organized the local Masonic lodge and served as its Master.

There was my grandfather, DeWitt, who grew up on the farm, but after graduating from Haverford School, decided on a business career. He went on to Pierce Business School, and then to work at Windsor Chocolates, a Philadelphia candy factory, where he became head shipper and met my grandmother, who worked as a general helper in packaging. She was from Lancaster; after her mother had died, her policeman father had deserted her, so she had been living with her grandfather, an ironmonger, before striking out on her own at age 16. I have a picture of her then, buxom and round-faced; she wears a long dress, puff-sleeved, in the style of 1900, with dark hair massed and piled on her head. They were married in 1904, and a year later, when she was pregnant, they moved back to the farm, settling in my great-grandfather's house, while my great-grandfather moved to a new house he had built down the road.

There was my father, also named John, born in 1906, followed by my two aunts, at four-year intervals.

My grandfather would walk three miles across the fields to Wayne each day and catch the Lancaster train for the ride into Philadelphia.

At 32, he became President of Windsor Chocolates, and then four years later the owners decided to sell. With money from my great-grandfather, bank credit, and money from the Windsor bookkeeper, who became a partner, my grandfather bought the Windsor equipment, rented space, and began the DeWitt P. Henry Company. After early hardships, including a disastrous fire, the company flourished in the post-war economy.

Then my great-grandfather died; the farm was divided up and sold (most of it would become the St. Davids Golf Club, where my family later dined and played), and my grandparents moved to Bloomingdale Avenue, then the finest street in Wayne.

My father spent his teenage years in that house, a boxy Victorian with a mansard roof, an open front and two side porches, and fifteen rooms. The yard was one acre, with a carriage barn and driveway in back, a low iron fence all around, and a variety of shrubs and tall shade trees. Before he could start at the Haverford School for Boys, he was stricken with osteomyelitis, a groove of infected marrow was taken from his left leg, and he was confined to bed for several months, but he studied with a tutor, and entered with his class spring term. At Haverford he worked his way back to physical and social confidence through sports, despite his permanently weakened leg and an embarrassing scar down the outside of his thigh, where folds of the incision had grown into the bone.

He did well academically, especially in chemistry, a field made glamorous in that era of discovery. His classmates were from families more established than his, and Haverford was meant to shape them for careers and colleges. Brains and breeding were assumed.

Thanks partly to a lodge brother of my grandfather's, he was accepted by Cornell, starting in the class of 1928. He played baseball and was rushed by Beta Theta Pi, where one of his fraternity brothers was Jerry Thralls, a lacrosse star, whose younger sister Kay was to become my mother.

Kay Thralls too was from a rising family, priding itself in privilege, though not as deeply rooted in place as the Henrys. Her father, Jerome, half-Irish, half-Welsh, was a self-made financier, who had been born on a Kansas chicken farm; while her mother, Ottalie, had been sent as an orphan girl from Germany to relatives in Kansas City, "with a tag around her neck." Jerome Thralls was working as a Wells Fargo driver and office agent when they had courted and married. My mother was born in 1907, with two older brothers, and then with a younger sister. Her father, meanwhile, was "advancing," starting his banking career with managing the Kansas City Clearing House and then moving the family to New York as he took a post with the American Bankers Association. During the war, he served in Washington as head of the Association's War Loan Organization, and, at war's end, left to found the Discount Organization of New York and become its senior officer. My mother had grown up in Brooklyn and was his match in intellect and will, and when he resisted her going to Cornell and having ambitions "in a man's world," she stood up to his bullying.

My father visited them as her brother's friend, and had his eye on Kay, even though he knew that she was dating someone else. When she left Cornell in mid-junior year (her married Classics professor kept making advances), and went on to art school in Manhattan, then switched to the Scudder School of Social Research and Secretarial Skills, she and my father only kept acquainted in a cheerful, off-hand way.

With campus recruiting, my father was hired to start as a research chemist at DuPont Chemical's Newark plant the fall after graduation. My father's parents gave him a summer's tour abroad for a graduation gift. He saw Paris ("very free and easy," he wrote home, "a lot of it would seem wrong in America, but it doesn't seem so terrible over here"), Versailles ("immense building, worth millions"), battlefields ("no large trees, thousands of graves"); he and a pal traveled to Italy, Genoa, Florence, Venice, Milan, Bellagio. He sent my mother a postcard from Florence. Then to Heidelberg, Germany; then to Brussels, where he caught a biplane to London (first in our family to fly, he wrote reassuringly, "it's safe and a regular thing over here").

Back home, he settled into a Newark apartment with other new grads; then sent my mother a postcard asking for a date. She had been living in Greenwich Village while going to Scudder and working as a volunteer, but now was back home in Brooklyn and reenrolled in art school, intending a career as an illustrator; and she had sold two drawings for a Macy's ad. They dated through that fall and winter, and all around them New York was booming. Skyscrapers were going up in mid-Manhattan; the Empire State Building was just beginning. Come spring, my father proposed.

My mother had been to Wayne and met the Henrys, and my grandmother Henry had ordered the engagement ring. DeWitt thought my father's DuPont job was a dead end ("You can't support a family on $35 per week!") and offered him a job in the candy factory starting at $50. Given the idea that he would learn the business and take over later, and with my mother happy to leave New York, my father agreed. They found a house in Ardmore. My father started at the factory, and while my mother summered with her family, he wrote her that she should come down and they "could have each other— Rather, be with each other, no having until October" (she would be a virgin, she later told me, on their wedding night). She did come down with her father, who got along with DeWitt, but privately labeled my grandmother "a stuffed shirt." Because he had to make a speech in California on the intended wedding date (he was setting up a foreign trade corporation), they moved up the wedding date a month and had a small family wedding in New York, instead of the big wedding my mother had planned.

For a honeymoon, my parents stayed in Ocean City, where they took their pictures in a boardwalk photo-booth (my father in a fedora and a camelhair coat; my mother in a fur and velvet cap; both clowning together and in love), and within four weeks my mother was pregnant with my brother, Jack. Then came October 29, Black Tuesday, and the stock-market crash. My grandfather Thralls was seriously affected, but they were only dimly aware. They had their own lives now.

*

From the time of selling the Henry farm and moving to Bloomingdale, my grandmother Martha aspired to join high society—a dream conditioned perhaps by issues of *Godey's Lady's Book* and the romance novels that she collected (these were later passed down and filled the sun-porch library shelves in our St. Davids house). My grandfather on the other hand, dwelt on business dreams, as the candy magnate and family patriarch (at his factory office, for instance, hung a large sepia photograph of himself as President). In any case, the Main Line had its social tradition. The Biddles, the Wannamakers, the Pews, the Adrossians: the very rich guarded family connections, and the social register, like that of gentry in England, protected standards of breeding, education, and fortune. In terms of stratification, the Henrys were nouveau upper-middle, seeking upper.

Whatever my grandmother thought of my father's match with the Thralls family, she put her primary hopes in my Aunt Peggy, the family beauty and "the belle of Wayne," who came out as a debutante and met, through her roommate at Dana Hall School, the sportsman and millionaire playboy Gail Borden, of the Borden's Milk Bordens. He hunted big game, collected guns, and flew his own small plane; he was also an expert skater who practiced figure skating regularly as Sonja Henie's partner in the New York Skating Club.

He and my aunt had a whirlwind romance. Then my grandmother invited him to Wayne, and went all out to impress him. She hired servants and kitchen help; repainted, redecorated, and refurnished the house; landscaped the yard, and put in a rose garden and trellis. She arranged formal dinner-, bridge- and garden-parties to introduce him to Main Line society. Shortly after my parents had settled in Ardmore, she staged a gala at the Penn Athletic Club to announce Peggy's engagement. Peggy and Gail were married in June, 1930, with a reception afterwards in the Warwick Hotel, and then left for a European honeymoon.

Jack was born shortly after they left. A film from the next Easter, when Gail brought his movie camera along, shows Jack, blond and gleeful, bouncing in a seat suspended from a spring, my father lean, my mother as always waving away the camera, and Aunt Peggy flaunting and preening in a fur and teasingly kissing my father on the front porch.

*

My parents had no social life outside of the Henry clan. My grandmother kept up her airs so unbearably that my other aunt, now seventeen, would run to my parents to escape her. Martha insisted that my parents come to the Wayne Presbyterian Church each Sunday, all line up in the family pew, and then come to dinner afterwards; and when my mother complained, my father told her, "You got trapped."

My father himself felt trapped at the factory. The Depression was worsening. There were unemployment, bread lines, bank closings, suicides (my grandfather Thralls nearly lost everything paying back investors after his brokerage partner jumped out a window). The Henry Company was in trouble as well. But just at that point, the Walter Baker Company's chief chemist was sent down from Boston on a troubleshooting visit—Baker was our chocolate supplier and there had been problems with a shipment. The chemist got to know my father, and told him that Baker had an opening. The prospects were outstanding. On his next trip down, the chemist made an offer, my father accepted, and my grandfather told him to go; whatever would happen to the Henry Company would happen anyway.

*

Those Walter Baker years, from 1932 through 1939, proved to be liberating, heady, and perhaps the happiest of their marriage.

My father began as "General Assistant on Coating and Cocoa Producing, Development, and Sales Service" for $3500. The Baker complex, located on the Neponset River in Dorchester covered eighteen acres, with fifteen interconnected buildings, a railroad depot, and the river winding through. There were eight hundred employees and the air smelled of chocolate for miles around.

My father worked in the main laboratory at first, testing products, and researching new formulas and products. A constant problem was fat bloom—a graying of chocolate, formed of surface crystals of fat exuded from it. When my father did chance upon a new technique for preventing bloom (he had been experimenting at home on my mother's stove), it caused a stir among the higher-ups.

They sent him on the road, on trouble-shooter and sales trips throughout the East. He was promoted with a raise. He mixed socially with the top executives, who were cultured, genial men, ten to twenty years his senior. He learned to play golf on public courses, then joined a four-some with the Merchandising Manager and the Sales Manager (who claimed Mayflower ancestry) at their private club in Milton. Later my parents were invited to dinner at the executives' homes, where my mother was popular. He admired and emulated these men. In 1935, he was appointed Assistant Sales Manager for the Midwest and South, which meant a transfer to the Chicago office of General Foods and another relocation for our family.

My brother Charles had been born in January, 1933; they'd moved to a new house in Newton, where my sister, Judith Ann, was born in February, 1935 and Jack started kindergarten. Now they moved to Western Springs, Illinois, and again to a larger house in Hinsdale. Each time my mother organized the moves, packed, unpacked, contracted with movers, house hunted, made and forsook friends, arranged for the schools. She kept the household accounts. She made all her own clothes and most of the children's. She took the children out. She cleaned, laundered, shopped, cooked, gardened, got into volunteer work, and always stood solidly behind my father: listened to his problems, made suggestions; helped him write reports. She even walked around with him as he practiced golf, the way she used to on Long Island with her father.

Before long, another promotion brought them back to Boston and a house on Chestnut Street in Newton. My brothers were in school. My father didn't have to travel as much. He now had staff and regional assistants under him. He also worked and traveled often with Curt Gager, the Merchandising Manager and Vice President of General Foods, who devoted his entire time now to the Walter Baker Company. Family to family, the Gagers became my parents' friends. Gager had worked his way up over fifteen years from sales assistant to sales manager at Maxwell House, and then from one job to another with General Foods, proving his talents. My father felt that he was on a similar path, and that Gager was grooming him to someday take his place, as Gager was in line for President.

*

From Wayne, they heard first that my aunt had divorced Gail, partly at odds with his skating crowd, but mainly because she couldn't have children, and Gail had refused to adopt. Next they heard that she had sailed to London, rekindled the romance, and remarried him. Once settled in Bethel, Connecticut, she and Gail visited Boston, where Gail was in a skating exhibition, and my aunt had asked my parents for my brother Chuck—she could do so much more for him than they ever could—but my mother had said no, sorry, as if it were a joke.

During these years, my father also heard regularly from his father. The Henry Company was at an impasse. My grandfather needed either to invest new money and expand or get out right away and salvage what he could. He decided to expand, mortgaged everything, and moved into a modern, efficient plant—some 45,000 square feet—in Germantown. Then in 1936, the union arrived. There was a three-week strike, and my grandfather was forced to recognize the union and sign a contract, something he never quite got over, convinced that the union could never do as well by the employees as he had always done himself. He felt betrayed. His older department heads had trouble too, adjusting from the old school of ruling by tempers and abuse, to the new, by reasoning, firmness, and supervision. The hardest blow, however, came with the sudden death of the company's vice president in 1938 (he had served as plant manager and had been part-owner since the beginning). My grandfather also learned of his own heart problems.

He asked my father to come home. In so many words, he told my father: "The family needs you. There's no one else. You have the training and experience. I wouldn't be asking, if it weren't a good opportunity. You'll be running the whole thing. I'll step aside. You can move right into Bloomingdale—we'll give it to you. Think about it. Talk it over. You've got a good job there, and you've put a lot into it, but this will be good too. You owe it to us, son. There's too many people depending on this. I'm not just asking for me."

My father consulted Curt Gager, seeking some guarantee if he chose to stay with the Baker Company, but all that Gager could say was that my father had potential. Nobody could promise anything. Besides, other Baker executives owned stock in the company, and that would be a serious factor for top level jobs.

My father doubted that he had the drive to succeed at that level. What if he let the Henry Company go, only to find himself stuck, finally, in some middle-level job? And at home, could my grandfather ever really step aside, poor health or no? My mother left it up to him; it was his career.

*

They moved back to Wayne on January 31, 1939.

My brothers ran ahead through the gate at Bloomingdale, as if for a holiday visit, followed by my mother and Judy, and then my father last. My grandfather lifted up Judy, then nodded at my father and clasped his hand. My grandmother gave her busses and hugs. Small talk, an exchange of keys. Then my grandparents headed back to their new apartment, leaving my parents to their work.

There must have been an oddness being home, physically. Where other houses had been blank slates, here memory colored everything. My grandmother left most of her furnishings for them to look after. There were the neighbors my father had grown up with. There were tradesmen with long-standing relationships to the family. My mother needed a maid, so my parents kept my grandmother's maid. Cyrus Truxel was the family doctor. Henefer, the dentist, was down the street. They joined the church now as a family. My father joined the St. Davids Golf Club and played on the Henry farm's former pasture (the house my father had been born in stood right behind the tenth green). My brothers started at the Haverford School. My mother joined the Saturday Club, Neighborhood League, and Red Cross, and my father took his place with the Masons.

Each weekday, my father picked up my grandfather and drove him in to the factory. The hour's commute took them through wooded areas with winding roads, past estates with mansions standing back, through business and residential areas, past a gravel quarry, over the Schuykill river and into the crowded, poor sections of Manayunk and

Germantown: tenements, row-houses, storefronts, taverns on every corner, and mainly immigrants, German, Swede, Irish, Greek (there were Orthodox Churches with minarets). The streets were paved with bricks or cobblestones from Revolutionary days.

"DeWitt P. Henry, Confectioners," a brass plaque announced beside the front door. A self-contained, two-floor building at 4837-9 Stenton Avenue, Germantown, the factory had banks of windows on all four sides; a steam plant out back, with its industrial chimney; and a large parking lot, which they could build on to expand. All the machinery was new and there were spacious refrigerated rooms for the packaging. The front office was modern and roomy. There were 150 employees. At this point, the company was worth some $400,000 in capital and operated on a one-million-dollar budget.

My grandfather held fifty-four percent of the stock, his brother twelve percent, and the former vice-president's estate held the rest. My father needed to buy shares from the vice-president's widow to consolidate his position, and my grandfather, already deeply in debt, couldn't help; so my father was forced to take out bank loans for an initial eleven-percent of the stock. His starting salary was eight thousand, compared to my grandfather's twelve thousand.

In business matters, my father respected DeWitt, but he knew he had the better executive skills and a better grasp of the industry and of national sales. He argued for diversifying their product line, investing in advertising, and developing a market name, but my grandfather refused to listen. They made their money from bulk goods, penny candies and gift assorteds. Their future was as a supplier, period.

Tensions grew between them at home as well as at work. This was my grandparent's world, not my father's. He felt like here he would always be the Henry boy, no matter what his own accomplishments. Visiting Bloomingdale regularly, my grandmother watched my mother's performance as a mother, cook, and hostess; while my mother privately ground her teeth. My grandfather would settle into a favorite chair, reflecting: "Nice to have my grandchildren around for a change.... These boys will be heirs to the company someday.... This was a good house for a family.... Just don't see what you young fellas get out of chasing that little white frustration around five miles of cow pasture." As for war breaking out between England and Germany, he swore by the isolationist creed: "It's not our fight. We're safe here. We're beating the Depression." My father worried about a peacetime draft and FDR's determination to get us in. What would that mean for the business or the family?

My grandparents quit their apartment and leased a small farm in Malvern, where my parents could visit, and the families could have more breathing room. My grandfather went into semi-retirement, still working half-days and keeping his office, while he made my father President in 1940.

For my mother's "birthday present," my father proposed having a fourth child, which my mother had been wanting. He had missed out on the early years of the others, he said, and being settled now, wanted to try his hand at real fathering. Once my mother was pregnant, my sister hoped for a sister, and my grandfather insisted that another boy, this time, be named for him. I was born June 30, 1941.

*

My grandparents moved again, this time to an elegant stone colonial house on six acres in nearby Ithan, which would be their permanent retirement home, and where, in January, 1941, at age 59, my grandfather had his first serious heart attack, throwing the fate of the business and the entire family's welfare suddenly onto my father.

Also by early 1941, months before Pearl Harbor, industry had entered a wartime economy, which meant new restrictions on candy as a "non-essential" industry. Cocoa beans and other raw materials were scarce. Sugar was rationed. No new machinery or replacement parts were available. If not the draft, then defense jobs took away most existing help, leaving my father shorthanded. In the midst of struggling with responsibilities that DeWitt had kept to himself (such as dealing with the banks), my father had to get through the war years. Fortunately, he was 4F because of his leg. DeWitt made him promise never to sell out the company or to liquidate. The only course was to run a skeleton operation and wait the war out.

We have our first home movies from that Easter, footage of my grandparents entering their Ithan home, of my mother pregnant, and of my sister Judy, and brothers Jack and Chuck, whose heads pop up with waggling fingers as the camera pans the elaborate garden.

*

My father's drinking problem began with his keeping a case of ale on ice. After openly drinking one bottle at dinner, he'd sneak an extra later. He'd stop alone at taprooms when he was out on errands. Later, he'd hide extra cases in the basement. He'd tiptoe down and sneak back in the coal bins to finish off one or two bottles. He was often drunk at home, nodding in his chair, listening to the radio. He'd been passed out when Jack had appendicitis, so that my mother had had to drive Jack to the hospital herself. Out for bridge, or with his foursome after golf, social drinking led to one too many, and before long old friends were avoiding him. When my mother confronted him, he told her he had a right to relax. He did his part. What did she want? Look what she had; look around!

He thought he could stop when he wanted. He was never hung over. His problem wasn't drinking, it was my mother's nagging, her hurt silences and looks; her suspicions.

The problem was the new baby crying in their bedroom annex, crying at all hours.

Drinking helped. It kept him with the family. A few drinks, and he felt as if ambition still had hope, as if he still were in his prime. Other times, drinking helped him blow off steam. He did his best. He kept on going on.

Before long, he had switched to harder stuff, hiding pints around the house.

*

The year after Pearl Harbor, all the victories were Axis. Papers warned of bombings. Blackout drills began. Air wardens were named. Rationing boards were set up. My father served on the local board as a volunteer. My mother dug up the remains of my grandmother's rose garden and planted a Victory Garden—the only one in our neighborhood—and eventually was feeding half of Lenoir Avenue. My brother Jack started raising chickens in the upstairs of the garage and selling their eggs. When my mother wasn't in the garden, she was in the kitchen boiling vegetables for canning, plucking chickens, saving fats.

My mother's brothers were all in the service. Two were officers on aircraft carriers; one was in the Air Force and designing secret bombsights at Princeton. Shortly after her younger sister's husband went into the Secret Service, the sister moved down with her baby and took an apartment to be near my mother. My mother's father moved to Washington to take a key post in the RFC, loaning out billions for war production, and rubbing shoulders with Jones, Hopkins, Forrestal, and even FDR.

The uniforms, the sermonizing, the newsreels and fireside chats, the harping on our boys, who were paying the supreme sacrifice: the more the country pulled together, the more my father felt left out.

What about his sacrifice? Who recognized, or even fathomed it?

DeWitt now picked up my father each morning in the old Buick, car-pooling to save gas, drove him in, puttered with paperwork and rested on his office couch all day, then drove him home; and DeWitt's presence, monitoring his every move, and maybe even guessing about his drinking, got to him.

The lectures: "I can understand you're frustrated. You think I've liked it? What about back after the fire? I had a rough road myself, but I stuck to it. Now we've got this war." The harangues: "You've always been a momma's boy. This is life. This is how it is. No one's asking you to like it."

My father suffered this in silence, as he suffered DeWitt's ordering him around in front of others at work; or at home, as he suffered the growing bond between DeWitt and Jack, aged twelve, whom DeWitt took in alone now Saturdays to the plant.

Morals were a joke. Birthrights and breeding were a joke.

As the tide of war changed, he tried to cut back his drinking, but nothing could settle his nerves the next day but another drink. He drank away from home and came home loaded. He thought he hid it from the children, his parents, and the outside world (he drank in lower-class taverns where he was anonymous). Not even my mother realized how much he drank.

In the privacy of their room late at night, and as my mother lay exhausted, turned away in bed, he'd be sitting up and drinking brazenly in front of her. Yeah, look, here I am. A man you never bargained for, huh? A man who wants his father dead. Think of that. Why not? You can crush a baby's skull, like a melon. Like that! You can bomb big cities. Dresden. V2s. Look at me! This is another person, here. No more decency. Look at Peggy. Think my mother cares? Gets divorced again. Shacks up with some electrician in Bethel. Gail, Jesus; Gail renounces worldly goods, joins the Holy Rollers, gives her a million bucks, anyways. S'joke. She goes to Florida, she meets some clerk, penniless, in the hotel. They get married and adopt a kid. She lends my parents money for Ithan. Suddenly, anything she does, it's okay. Guest of honor, back in the fold. Clerk goes 'n ships off to the Army. Take your big shot Curt Gager. You always liked him, huh? Model citizen, old wonderful Curt, big family man. Shoulda seen him carry on. Strip joints, floozies. Sex was everywhere. All these kids, these bobbysoxers.

Finally, my mother had enough: "John, I'm tired of listening. I have children to take care of. You have to pull yourself together or get out."

"Get out? Whose house is this?"

He wrestled her downstairs in her slip and locked her outside. Jack had to come and let her in.

Another time, he hit her hand away. He threw his glass at her across the room.

Days after the images haunted him. He'd be playing catch, and when he looked at his sons, there would be the vision of their faces saucer-eyed the night before. He'd been shouting, breaking things. No. He'd blink and there would be the day itself, continuing. Or if he couldn't blink it all away—the powdered-over bruises; a hard glance or curtness from my mother; the stain on the wall, the broken clock or lamp—he'd need another drink.

The war wound down. FDR died and Truman was President. At the factory, they got a defense contract for C-rations and then a canteen contract for nut chews, so things looked up. They built on the annex, allowing them to do their own warehousing and shipping from the plant. VJ Day came after the bombs on Japan. Soldiers started coming back.

Then DeWitt died suddenly, July 9, 1946. He had been shaving in his rented cottage at Ocean City, when he just keeled over. Hundreds of friends—business associates, fellow Masons, church friends, Wayne friends, all the old-timers from the factory, my mother's family—sent flowers and cards or attended the big memorial service; but the funeral itself was just for family. The *Suburban and Wayne Times* carried his obituary, celebrating his prominence and remembering him as "the son of the late Mr. and Mrs. John Henry, who were among the earliest settlers in this vicinity."

*

The girl, Ida, had started as a secretary at the factory in 1945. Her family lived in Germantown, an older brother in the Army in the Pacific, a younger still in school; her mother worked in a rubber plant; her father, a metal worker, had walked out on them some years back. She was seventeen. She had been dating sailors since she was fourteen.

Immediately, she drew my father's eye: black hair up in elaborate hairdos, baring her neck; lipstick; frilly blouses, tight skirts, high heels. She teased him with an undercurrent of recognition: "Oh, Mr. Henry, shame!" Or "You're not so old." She told him about her dates, her romances, her disappointments with young boys. She liked a good time. She went to bars. She had her own apartment. He'd drive her home after work and they'd stop for drinks. Away from prying eyes, she'd take his hand, or walking, slip an arm around his waist. Once, turning in a doorway, she brushed him with her breasts, so he felt their softness. In the car, they kissed, and he was careful, later, to clean off the lipstick.

She was possible. She was discreet. She looked up to him. She listened to his troubles and sympathized. She saw his side against my mother and his home life, and she mocked his bad conscience: how was the weekend? How was dinner? She could have boys my brothers' ages, with slim muscled bodies and carefree lives, but she chose him. He told her about his single life, his fraternity days. He even asked my mother to find his Beta pin, so he could give it to Ida.

He moved into his father's big office, promoted Ida to his private secretary and built a private office for her, even though the plant manager objected and told him that he should get somebody to work, not play. They were lovers by then and he didn't care what people thought. He was President.

Ida called him openly at home; the affair became reckless.

He woke beside her one morning, not having meant to stay the night. Her bedroom, her apartment. His head throbbing. Sounds of semis, diesels, chirping birds; first light beneath the shades. She lay with her bare back to him, smooth and flawless. As he came back from the shower, she had turned over naked, sheet thrown back, pleading, "Love me, love me again, Johnnie."

AWOL, he didn't care. Hell with work. Hell with home. Nobody's business.

She didn't mind his scar, his graying hair or weight. With excited tenderness, she touched and felt the folds in his leg, the flesh deep in as sensitive as his navel's.

My mother turned to Dr. Truxel. She broke her code of silence and told him about the drinking, which my father took as a betrayal, but Dr. Truxel persuaded him to listen. He was sick. Look at the damage he was doing to himself, to my mother, to all of us. Beginning in 1947, Dr. Truxel got my father to work with a man from A.A. He also sent my father to the detox unit of the Pennsylvania Institute, where he was treated by the Chief Psychiatrist, Kenneth E. Appel, who specialized in alcoholism. My father lived there for brief stretches, in and out.

He kept an alcoholic's diary. He meditated on the Twelve Steps. He was wary of A.A. meetings, even though his sponsor insisted that alcoholism was an illness and that many respectable people were afflicted with it. He read books about the disease. He had his therapy.

Talk weaknesses and strengths. Talk immaturity. Talk when he felt like drinking, what the costs had been in the past. Talk what there is in life that is satisfying, aside from booze. Talk pride in supporting the clan. Pride in being loved. Pride in business friends and their regard. Pride in his children. Pride in my mother's loyalty, caring for him for his own sake. Pride in doing right by his children in education and upbringing. Pride in his comforts and possessions, his TV, his Buick, his flowering yard. Pride in his second chance. Try to understand the patterns: overprotective mother, distant and over-authoritarian father, preventing him from developing maturity. Maturity was stick-to-itness and the ability to accept and practice a dependency on God. Appel told him that he was trying to make his wife into his mother, and that she refused to be his mother because she was mature.

*

A year later, however, Dr. Appel told my mother that my father had so many hang-ups, it wasn't worth the effort. She should let him go.

He was drinking again, home that Christmas Eve. He loved Ida and she wanted to marry him. As he yearned for her, and as he brooded on starting over, the family commotion assaulted him: cooking smells, excited voices, clickings, rattling doors. Everybody happy. He felt himself an outsider in his own life. Just then carolers came up the walk, singing, "Tis the season to be jolly!" He was out of his chair, out the storm porch, door open, blast of cold, yelling: "Outta here, off my walk, outta my yard!" And Jack came behind him, "Okay, okay, Dad. C'mon, I'll take care of it."

My mother had come, and Chuck. They called the A.A. man. My father went into the Institute the next day.

Later he told my mother he couldn't take anymore. He wanted a divorce. He had decided to move out.

"I've ruined this family and want to start another one."

"Fine," my mother told him. "Not now. Dry out first."

At the golf club, already drunk, he found the locker room door locked, and went around to the ornate front entrance. Some guy, wife in tow, was just coming out from dinner. "Hello, John." A shocked face. "Little under the weather, fella?" My father pushed on into the grill and bar. Who were these men? This was his turf, literally. Who's that dope in the Army uniform? Big fuss. Nothing. Signifying nothing. Play at Haverford. Bad man conscious of his villainy, huh? Know what it feels like? Pain, goddamn it. Rage. Wanting to be helpless, wanting power; then plunging deeper, farther, like a ghost, apart from life, unaccountable and drifting at will, reveling in impunity the way that war criminals must, above and beyond all decency and law—wrongly so, yet blamelessly too.

He couldn't stand the sight of us, and especially of me, the baby. "Get him out of here! I don't want to look at him!"

This life was finished.

He'd burned bridges.

Jack drove him into Philadelphia, to the Warwick Hotel. Jack was eighteen and had flunked out of his first semester at Cornell, where he had wanted to be an engineer or architect, anything but working with my father at the factory. They had no secrets. Both were spent.

"Here you are." No handshake. No hug. "Here's your bag." The Warwick overhang, the doorman. "So long," Jack said abruptly, then got in and drove off around the corner, never looking back.

He checked in. He sat up in his room, about to call Ida. He needed a bottle; was swallowing, suddenly gripped with thirst. No. He saw and felt it on his hands, like blood, sticky and indelible. His hand hitting my mother. His hands smoking. He wasn't strong enough to start over. He thought suicide. Lacked nerve. After lost minutes, his hand lifted, reaching as heavily for the telephone as for a gun.

"Number please?"

His voice was steady and businesslike: "Wayne 0774."

"Thank you."

The ring, ring; then my mother's cheery, public greeting, "Yes?"

Heart beating, eyes clenched, "Come get me," was all he said.

*

I can only imagine this John Henry. I search for him in Wayne and its history; in the local newspaper accounts; in letters and journals;

in public records; in household artifacts; in photographs and home movies; and in studies of alcoholism. I search for him in his own accounts to me and in the accounts, often conflicting, of my mother, my brothers and sister. In midlife now myself, I search for him in the alcoholic breakdowns of close friends. I search for him in tests of my own mettle as a man, a husband, and a father.

The John Henry I grew up with never had another drink. He stayed with us. He stayed with the factory. He broke things off with the girl, who left the factory, married and moved to Altoona. After offering each of us a chance to succeed him at the factory, years later he negotiated the sale of the Henry Company to Pet Foods, which owned Whitman's Chocolates, and then retired.

He loved and idolized my mother, and concluded his personal account of his "bad time" to me when I was seventeen: "Your mother stuck with me through that. A lot of women wouldn't have, couldn't have, and I'll always be grateful to her for that. We should all be grateful. She's one woman in a thousand." He would shout at me red-faced at the slightest sign of disrespect towards her.

He supported our turns at college (Jack dropped out, Judy got married, Chuck went on to medical school, I went for a PhD), and ultimately our moves away. He loved us through changing times and changing mores from the 1950s into the 1970s. Where we all rejected the Main Line's pretensions, he clung to appearances and basked in material privilege. He suffered our mocking and our fat-man jokes. His golf club friends and business friends knew nothing of his past. He rehearsed, gloated and boasted of what he believed to be our happy outcomes.

His favorite song, sung hoarsely in good spirits, had the line, "Looking through the knothole in my father's wooden leg." Originally it was a camp song, and he must have picked it up as a teenager, but I wonder to this day whether he savored the irony of this nonsense song's alluding to his own father's flaws, and the chance of independent vision based upon them—the hard-won adult truth that only by seeing through your father's weakness and by admitting to his humanity can you claim your life.

Long-Distance

When Connie answered the phone, then mouthed, "Chuck," I groaned inwardly. Another one- or two-hour conversation, at his expense (in those days, fifty-cents per minute), impossible to close. Politics was the minefield. He would bait and goad Connie, as my father had, and then debate her. He would tell me get off the phone; I'm talking to your wife.

I tried to veer from serious talk in our conversations to some mockery or absurdity that had us both laughing. The family reunion talk, for instance. Chuck on his return from Europe—he and his "fiancée" Maureen had flown on the Concorde—wanted to trace our family tree in Ireland and thought we should all meet there. He would pay the way. I kidded that we should trace our origins back to the Druids and meet at Stonehenge and that set us both off howling.

Before and after Mom's death, he had helped me to accept our secondary infertility and had supported Connie's pursuit of international adoption. He had followed the news of our choosing the Korean program, and going to Korean culture classes. The night our infant son David arrived, Chuck called, demanding, "How do you feel? Tell me how you feel." All I could say was that I felt proud, larger, that life would be different. I couldn't tell him that I was still grieving my infertility, and that life, in fact, felt overwhelming to me.

*

Both my parents held up Chuck to me as an example. When I visited them from college or graduate school, they drove me into Philadelphia on the Expressway, and then across Walt Whitman Bridge to Chuck's for Thanksgiving or Christmas dinner. For my mother, he was a doctor, serving humanity; for Dad he was rich, respected, and the family man. Especially as I persisted in my own unorthodox dreams (unpublished writer, unemployed PhD), as I put off marriage, and then when I was married, I put off having children, I viewed Chuck's life with intimidation and chagrin.

He had married Nancy, who was my age, while he was still interning at Bryn Mawr Hospital, where she was taking a nursing degree. They had lived in a residents' apartment; Chuck Jr. was born there in 1964. Then Chuck took a surgical practice in Woodbury, N.J. He bought a starter house in Wenonah. Two more sons were born, Bob in 1965 and Scott in 1967. He worked maniacally, always on call. Then they bought the rangy Victorian house in Woodbury, much like the house we had grown up in. This was the house that vas had built, Chuck would joke, since sterilization by snipping the *vas deferens* was in steady demand.

*

He was a dedicated, gifted surgeon by all accounts. Before long he had moved from partnership to his own practice. He loved telling Mom and Dad about his cases. I granted him that center to his life, though I knew practically nothing about it. I assumed he was meticulous, intuitive, and deft. He saved lives. He improved the quality of life for others, where other doctors had failed. Some patients he cared about personally and grieved when he lost them. And he was always proud and ready to help our family with any medical questions or issues.

After Jack had married, one of his three adopted children needed an operation and Chuck brought her east and performed the surgery himself. On the rare occasions when he touched me as a doctor, he was confident and gentle, fingering my throat for any signs of an enlarged thyroid, for instance. His practice was before computers. He prided himself as a diagnostician with a sixth sense. When Connie was pregnant, one of his jokes was to insist that by looking behind her ears, he knew the sex of our child, but he would refuse to tell us. After the birth, of course, he said, "See I was right. I'm never wrong."

*

His favorite novel, Chuck always said, was *Magnificent Obsession* by Lloyd C. Douglas, a 1929 pot-boiler about a dedicated doctor and anonymous philanthropist, later made into a film. Its playboy hero was saved from a boating accident, but at the cost of emergency care being denied to a beloved local doctor, who was having a heart attack. The playboy decides to devote his life to making up for loss of the doctor's life by becoming a doctor himself. About his own vocation, Chuck told me later that he had always wanted to be a doctor. As a boy he had healed a bird's broken wing; at fifteen, with Mom's blessing, he had followed around our family doctor on house calls. When he had broken his hand playing baseball, the surgeon who saved his hand had helped him to get a job in the cast room at Bryn Mawr hospital, and then had let him wash up, stand in, and watch operations. This contrasted to my own memory of his making his career choice only after he had returned from his Army tour in Korea in 1957, and even then after he had first shown a portfolio of drawings to a commercial artist, asking whether he could make a living by art. The artist had discouraged him, and at that point Chuck had turned to medical school. He meant to use his gifts for the good of others. He wanted to return to Korea, he had told us then, or perhaps to other Asian countries as an Albert Schweitzer. He had wanted to serve unselfishly in places of epic poverty and need, but then this idealism had been checked by Nancy's pregnancy and their marriage.

*

Following our father's death in 1976, Chuck's family life fell apart. He separated from Nancy in 1982, and got his divorce three years later, awarding Nancy one million dollars. Mom was glad for Chuck, whatever the price. Nancy had been a terrible mother and wife, Mom told me now. Nancy had hated having children and told her sons so.

At 20, 19 and 17, the boys had problems with drugs and alcohol. Their futures worried Chuck.

Then Mom fell ill with degenerative heart failure. Over her last six months, Chuck was the mainstay, not only keeping in close touch with her heart specialist, but also visiting as often as possible. Connie and our daughter Ruth stayed with her for two months, while I went back and forth from my teaching. Judy, then Jack took turns staying with her through that summer. She was hospitalized a number of times, the last time in a private room where we visited once. Otherwise we called long-distance to her bedside phone, and Chuck called us later to keep us updated. One visit he waltzed with her, he said, and the nurse rushed in when her monitor fell off. Finally Chuck told us that she had had enough. The medicine that prolonged her life only kept her in pain, so she chose to stop taking it. She would have a few more days. I called and said goodbye. Then Chuck called and told me that she was gone.

Each of us was wounded by her loss, but none so much as Chuck, I think now.

Chuck took on the role of her executor. After the funeral, he had us go through the house, dividing keepsakes. Being within driving distance, Connie and I made two or three trips down and met Chuck at the house. Mom had given me her Buick La Sabre that summer when my car had died in her driveway and had to be towed away, and now we loaded it to the ceiling. Chuck must have shipped us the larger furniture later on. He also shipped paintings and other items to Jack and to Judy. Finally, Chuck had to oversee the estate auction on his own and spoke of the heartbreak, seeing strangers dicker over this or that, the house gutted. He had loaded his own car at the last minute with things he couldn't see go, including a stack of paintings in the basement. The house itself was on the market for more than a year.

*

After his divorce, Chuck had moved into a condo, which I first saw in 1988. I was attending a teachers' convention in Philadelphia, and Chuck drove over and picked me up to spend the final night. The condo was Chuck's statement of a new life, not only a life without Nancy, but now also a life without Mom. He seemed to be searching for the person he was without his marriage, and for Jack, Judy and me, in some way to fill the void. This was after I had published an essay about my childhood in an attempt to reclaim our family past and to come to terms with the pain surrounding Dad's alcoholism. Chuck was proud of my essay and told me he showed it around his office. He also had Judy's family album, reproductions of all the family pictures from the 1880s forward, which Judy had assembled for each of us from Mom's desk drawers. He treasured most of all Mom's art.

We entered a foyer, past golf bag and clubs, a bowling ball, umbrellas, then went down stairs into a two-story living room, with mirrored walls and shelves, and to the right a split level loft, and under that the kitchen, bathroom, and then down a hall, a study to the left, a dining nook to the right, where a ship model was in progress, and then his bedroom and closets. A huge leather couch faced an entertainment center and dominated the living room. An oversized TV—a rarity then—and state of the art of audio: receiver, turntable, tape deck, stereo speakers. A table in front of the couch and two matching easy chairs. On the walls everywhere, on the shelves, on the walls ascending to the loft and on the walls of the loft itself were Mom's paintings, including her largest, proudest oils that had hung before in her living room and bedroom. There were also some of Chuck's best pen-and-inks, of Korean orphans, framed. There were several of my nephew John's etchings. Though homophobic, Chuck was as unequivocally proud of John's talent as Mom had been.

One of his sons or another sometimes stayed with him in the condo, so that making up the bed on the split-level loft was part of a ritual. Food was microwaved, bought at a 7/11 down the street. There was little in the refrigerator other than beer. Everything seemed orderly and spruce otherwise, so I assumed that a maid came in each week.

He took me to his office in a professional building nearby, with a view of a parking lot and fields. He had a secretary. He was loved by his patients, and deferred to by associates, though he complained of paperwork and hospital politics. Increasingly he operated on cancers. He had the dream of someday discovering a cure for cancer, relying more on his intuition and experience than on research. He thought the culprit was the immune system somehow.

*

Long-distance, he shyly boasted that he was dating different women, so he "must still be doing something right." There was Irene, a wealthy Guatemalan, who worked for Federal Express, and whom he later visited in Guatemala City and kept in nightly contact with by telephone. There was a woman in New Hampshire, daughter of a doctor friend; he drove up to see her, stopping overnight with us first, the first time he had seen our house and my son David, who was four. He arrived looking stylish and dapper. He had always been a handsome man, naturally lean, a little taller than I was. He was driving a new Buick. He wore glasses and his hair was totally white. He was fifty-five.

We had built our family room addition, and there is a picture of David in his lap and wearing a dinosaur mask. Chuck slept on the couch. Connie as always was gracious. I think there was some wistful irony for Chuck that he was the lone wolf now, visiting us in our domestic life.

A year later he told us he had a special girlfriend, someone he had been dating regularly. Judy and her daughter Lucia were coming to New York to sell their dolls at a toy show. Connie's mother lived in Manhattan and we could stay there, while she looked after Ruth and David. Chuck proposed that we all go out to a show, expenses on him. He wanted us to meet his honey, Maureen Froman. He bought us all tickets to *The Phantom of the Opera*. He and Maureen took a suite at the Waldorf Astoria, and we met there for drinks first. Their fling seemed decadent to us, and even more so to Judy, who was preoccupied with the Toy Fair, and didn't have much time to socialize. The suite was showy, with antique, formal furniture, mirrors, bad paintings, thick white pile carpeting, and I recall a sunken hot tub in a bathroom larger than our own living room. We had caviar and champagne. Maureen in her late forties resembled a well-preserved Doris Day, Chuck's calendar girl as a teenager. They were each other's playmates. We caught a cab in the rain. The high-tech spectacle of *Phantom* was a shock. At a Broadway restaurant afterwards for late dinner, Maureen leaned over the table and asked Judy how long she and I had been married—a boozy gaffe, especially given our earlier introductions and the fact of Connie sitting beside me. We laughed it off, but when Judy called from back home in Pasadena, she singled out this moment as proof that Maureen was self-absorbed and shallow, another of Chuck's party girls.

*

He had been complaining regularly about malpractice insurance and the trumped-up suits that had been brought against him, but I was surprised when he called to announce that he had retired early at the age of 58. He was embittered and resigned. His life had been for others. If lawyers and bureaucrats had made it impossible for him to practice, then that wasn't his fault, it was just too bad. He had his honey, Maureen, and they were engaged, though both having been through divorces, they knew better than to ever get married. He would play golf. They would travel together. He had his golf, bowling, drinking, and fishing buddies, mostly doctors themselves. He was building model boats from complicated kits. Otherwise, he lived alone in his condo, and Maureen lived in hers. She had also retired and had independent means.

He told me about one patient, a woman on whom he had performed a mastectomy, and with whom he had joked, saying, "You are mine, now." When she heard about his retirement, she came to his office, enraged: "How could you do this? How could you leave me? I trusted you!" He said a lot of patients were angry with him and felt deserted.

I told him I thought it was a waste. That he had a gift, and that there must be some way to use it. You just can't turn away.

"Oh, yes I can," he said. "It isn't easy, but I can."

Nevertheless, at the invitation of a former intern and protégé, who now ran a hospital in Nairobi, he and Maureen traveled to Kenya in 1995, where he practiced surgery for six weeks as a volunteer, performing more than 300 operations. This fulfilled, in some sense, his early idealism. In addition to practicing at the hospital, he and Maureen played golf and toured. He spoke of a hot-air-balloon trip they had taken, and of the balloon landing accidentally over the border in a hostile country, but after a scary encounter with soldiers, they had taken off again. When he tried to express the fascination of Africa, he could only tell us to see that movie, *Out of Africa,* it's just like that. "Gee," he would say, as if it were a discovery, "they really know how to live life over there."

*

In 1992, having finished my first full-length attempt at telling our family history, I sent copies of the manuscript to Jack, Judy, and, with trepidation, to Chuck. There was silence for a while. Then Judy called to tell me that Chuck had called her, upset. And that he had also called Jack. She told him it didn't bother her, because it was just the way I saw things, given my younger-brother status. Jack had told him the same thing.

I did feel that we all had tried to deny Dad's breakdown and the near destruction of our family. The attempts to spare me a glimpse into this Bluebeard's closet had, in fact, traumatized me in a different way. I needed to understand the passions behind our family's pretense of normality. While loving Mom as the pillar of our family, and as the martyr, Judy saw Dad as a self-centered child, Jack saw him as responsible and to blame, and Chuck seemed torn, needing to see Dad as human, as intelligent, as a loving and dedicated family man. We each had our "tribal scars" (my book's title then) and I thought it was important for us each to admit and to confront them.

Besides stirring up memories that Chuck obviously had set to rest, my portrayal was critical of Chuck himself for his conservative politics, for his seeming racism, and for his materialism, while I idolized Jack for his humanity and nobility. Chuck must also have been troubled by my presuming to write without the mask of privacy, personal or familial, while he himself had attempted to maintain a happy picture both of our family and of his marriage and had prided himself on keeping the painful parts to himself. The one thing he did say to me about the book was that I should write thrillers and stay away from the family stuff. I replied that I could only write what I could write.

*

Chuck always got sappy when he spoke of Maureen, like a teenager with a crush. They traveled to Mexico, to Europe, to Myrtle Beach. They had fun. He never said much about her tastes, interests or opinions. She and he had agreed officially to be engaged, he would say, but indefinitely—he chuckled about this. They would never set a date. Maureen had neither children nor family, but she did have friends in common with Chuck. Over the years, I had no real impression of her beyond her being pretty, restless, and jealous of Chuck's time visiting family. They had visited us in Boston once since the New York encounter; just stopping by on their way to Vermont. I remember Maureen perched on the edge of one of Mom's couches, trying to be polite, but really not relating to our world.

Depending on how drunk or tired he was—he never spoke to me when he was incoherently drunk, as he did, apparently, when he called Judy—he would either ask me for advice, granting me wisdom as if I were Mom; or more frequently, he would slip into talking to me like one of his boys—even calling me Scott once—so that I needed to remind him, "I'm your brother, remember; not your son, Chuck." He did repeat himself often, circling around set themes or stories, as if he suffered from memory loss.

Over the years, I imagined him alone in that condo, working on a model ship (one time the knife slipped and he cut his hand); watching golf on TV; drinking vodka; barely eating. He would call Judy, Jack, me; then each of his sons; Maureen, when they were close; or the girlfriends from before. He went bowling with his doctor friends. He and his friends had collective haircuts, paying the barber to come to them. He went on golf trips. When he traveled he went with style.

But the condo itself had slipped into a place of reclusive retreat.

I bought him Richard Ford's 1995 novel *Independence Day* thinking that he might recognize something of his world in that story of a feckless New Jersey father, life-crossed, divorced, and trying to build a relationship with a young son. Besides the appeal of local color, I thought Ford's existentialism might appeal to him. But I doubt he ever got into it. He never mentioned it later.

In February 1996, he called and caught Ruth home from college while I was out. "Was he drunk?" she asked me tearfully later. I called him back. Chuck said that he and Maureen were to visit Colorado this weekend, but their flight had been canceled because of snow; he hadn't been able to get out his car with the condo cul-de-sac plowed in until today; he had lived three days on ice cubes, no food; today he had gone out and gotten cold cuts and bread and frozen dinners, but he had no appetite. He was worried about Jack. Actually Jack had called me the night before and sounded well, in good spirits and health. Chuck started telling me about his brotherly bond to Jack. He wanted to tell me the truth about the summer trip the three of us took back when, and which I had written about in my book. In his mind I had been eight or nine. I had no idea what was going on between him and Jack.

"Chuck, I've written about all this. It's there. I was 14. It was 1955, one year after Dad asked Mom a second time for a divorce. My understanding was that it was a parent-sponsored bonding between us as brothers, maybe to protect me. I have documented all this."

Chuck kept intimating that this was my imagination, not the facts, that something else was going on with him and Jack that I didn't know then and could not understand now. Of course, from my research, I knew that in the summer of 1955 Chuck was on leave from the Army before shipping to Korea. This was the same summer that Judy announced her pregnancy and married Hans; the same that Jack threatened to deck Chuck, when Chuck referred to Hans (who was half-Indonesian) with a racial slur. Later Dad flew with Chuck to Seattle for his departure to Korea, and on the way stopped in the Chicago airport, where Dad found himself standing in line for a urinal behind Adlai Stevenson in the men's room. "His was bigger than Adlai's," Chuck said now; then he returned, in the face of what I had written, to the truth that "Mom and Dad loved each other, only that," that this was what he saw in their visits to his home in New Jersey. I objected, no, "I lived in their frustration and hate, but life is complex that way. Mom did tell me that the night before Dad's jaundice attack, that she and he had been lovers."

Chuck said, "Don't get into me about Dad. He could have lived." At that point, he choked and broke down. I was embarrassed. This was the first sign of his vulnerability to me. I tried to comfort him: "You're not responsible, Chuck. I remember that story."

"Just remember," he said cryptically. "You are the product of pain."

*

In 1997, Chuck bought a time-share condo in Los Cabos, Mexico, where he wanted Connie and me to visit, but we never did. A paradise, he said, right on the edge of a golf course.

I kept him up on our news. My career struggles. My worries about Ruth at Hampshire College as well as her becoming her own person, worries that had led me to write an essay about her and to co-edit an anthology called *Fathering Daughters.* She was readying at age 20, in the face of our apprehensions, for five months alone in Guatemala, which would count as her junior year. I told him about Dave's finishing sixth grade at Connie's school and our search for private middle and upper schools. I told him about Dave's trouble in coping with the cancer deaths, first, five years before, of his eight-year-old best pal, and then of his best pal's father, in the fall of 1998; I told him about Connie's mother in New York also being diagnosed with cancer in the spring of 1998, and the toll on Connie and on all of us as she went through operations and chemo, leading to her death that winter. I told him about Dave's loving and needing me, and how lucky I felt to have a living son, a loving wife, and a capable daughter. I told him about my marathon training and running, which made him proud, he said, especially when he thought of all the years that I had suffered from rheumatoid arthritis.

I never told him, however, that for a number of years I had been depressed and drinking myself; or that I had been scared into quitting, when, with Connie and the kids away, I had blacked out and failed to meet a class for the first time. In fact, other than in my writing, I was wary of offering him real intimacies, for fear that he would pounce on the occasion to lecture and intrude himself. Mostly I just listened.

*

He talked about his sons, one by one, upbeat at first. Bob had dropped out of college in Florida, but he had joined the Navy, which was a good thing. Charles Jr. had married a stripper in Arizona and had two children. Scott had tried college in Virginia, then dropped out and bummed around back home; then had moved to Boston and after a brief stay with us, rented an apartment nearby and clerked at a convenience store while he took classes first at a community college, and then at U. Mass. Boston. But each hopeful development was soon followed by heartache and dismay. Bob was in the brig for drug addiction. Charles Jr. was divorced. Scott had been taking the money Chuck sent for rent and tuition and spending it on drugs. Then Bob was discharged from the Navy and settled in New Jersey to be near his mother. Scott had moved back to New Jersey and married the woman he had been seeing all along, Juana, who was poor, and lived with her three children at her mother's. Off and on Scott had stayed with them, hungry for the family love (I am guessing) that he had been denied. When Scott and Juana moved to San Antonio, Texas, and when Scott adopted the three children, and got a job as an Emergency Room orderly, Chuck helped them with the adoption expenses and the down payment for a house, and felt proud that Scott was settled. Meanwhile Charles Jr. had disappeared from the Tucson area, as had his ex-wife and the children. I couldn't follow the details, something about a court injunction and the children becoming wards of the state. My brother had hired a private detective to track down the children, but with no luck.

*

In early April 1998, Chuck called while Connie and David were out, and I was alarmed that he sounded suicidal. His closest golfing and fishing friend had died. He felt isolated, he said. He was always the one who initiated the calls to his kids, to his sibs. Why didn't I ever call him? He wanted to know about Ruth's progress in Guatemala and asked how I could let Connie go in two weeks to visit her. He knew the place. He knew it was dangerous. He loved Connie and she had saved my life from the jerk I was, but she was political and this was a political trip.

No, I said. He knew nothing about raising a daughter in today's culture.

He said he had raised a sister.

He said he resented my stereotyping him as a conservative or anything else. I laid all these attributes on him, but I had no idea who he really was.

There weren't many people in his life who gave it meaning, he said. His boys only contacted him for money and never said thanks. When he died, he would just sneak away.

The one thanks he had ever gotten was a letter from the hospital in Nairobi, which was probably a fundraising letter, but which acknowledged and thanked him for his service there.

He didn't know what he could do for his sons, for their own good. He had bailed them out of trouble far into their adult lives.

He had mentioned concerns about his estate before. He had all this money and he didn't know what to do with it after his death. He had our mother's art; and what would become of that? I had no room for it, nor did I want to pay for storage. He felt that the money would only ruin his sons. I had suggested several times that he talk to an estate lawyer and think about setting up trusts.

Despite his relationship with Maureen, he felt profoundly alone. Soon after this call, he told Judy that he was setting up a fund for the Memorial Underwood Hospital and cutting his sons off entirely, but she urged him to think of his grandchildren and their futures.

In any case, he was asking me now to be his executor. I told him, sure, of course. Think about it, he said.

He had no will, he said. The state of New Jersey had laws that depended on proof of blood claim. I didn't catch that, did I?

After a moment I asked: "You mean because Nancy was screwing around, you aren't sure the boys are yours?"

And then he shared the hard private news, at least in his own mind: only Chucky was his. The others looked like their fathers. Bobby's was a hairdresser.

He had come home one night in Wenonah and found Nancy's clothes all over the house and she was naked on top of this guy in the backyard and he had beaten up the guy and she'd tried to pull him off and it all had come out. There had been a doctor at Bryn Mawr also, and others.

What was he thinking in telling me this now? That if he died without a will that Chucky, on proof of blood claim, would get everything?

He had had similar conversations with Judy and with Jack, neither of who wished to serve as executor. Now he was asking me. Yes, I said, of course I would serve. I felt that I owed him my promise, based on his own service as our mother's executor.

We had another conversation that summer, when I was rehearsing my struggles to plan for paying off Ruth's college expenses, followed by the costs of private school for Dave and later his college. Chuck was shocked to hear that the going tuition rate was close to $30,000 for each of four years. He wanted to make sure that his grandchildren were provided for against future education costs.

Still later, in December, he outlined the arrangements to be drawn up in his will, and again asked me to serve as executor. I had asked him before, and asked him again now, pointedly, if he had any reason to worry about his health: "Is the Reaper at your door, Chuck? Be honest with me." After a moment's hesitation, he said no. In fact, he and Maureen were planning a trip. He was fine.

*

Judy called me in Boston from Pasadena in May 1999. Maureen had just called her from New Jersey and told her that Chuck was dying of lung cancer, and had been in the hospital for a week. Chuck hadn't wanted to tell anyone, Maureen said, but now we had to know. Also that Maureen had finally consented to marry Chuck and that they had had a ceremony in the hospital a few days ago. Judy said that she herself had then called Chuck at his hospital bed, and when she offered to fly cross-country to see him, he had said not to bother, that he wouldn't be here when she arrived.

I hesitated, but Connie insisted, fresh from the loss of her mother three months before: "We have to go," she said; "right now. You'll never forgive yourself if you don't try." Since there wasn't time for Jack and Judy to visit, I would stand as the sibling surrogate. We put our lives on hold–our children with friends—piled into our rickety van, just the two of us, and drove the seven hours from Boston. Chuck was in the hospital in Woodbury, New Jersey, where he had served for years, and where the attending doctors, staff, and nurses all treated him with deference, one of their own.

We could only visit for two days, overnight. Though he was close to the end, he had perhaps weeks left (three, it turned out). He was himself, lucid, ironic. He had complained different times that we never visited. "Well, here we are," I told him. "That was so simple, driving down."

And he replied, "Yeah, but look what it took to get you here."

*

He was in a private room with two beds. From the bed near the windows, and cranked up to a sitting position, he watched a TV mounted overhead. The other bed had the photo albums of Chuck and Maureen's trips stacked up, opened. Vases and baskets of flowers were on the dresser and the windowsills and a table beside his bed. He was gaunt and enfeebled, stomach breathing. He wore pajama bottoms, but no top. Pillows were stacked behind his back and head. He had monitor wires, an IV and oxygen tubes; as he breathed from a nose clip, he needed a cotton pad, like a mustache, for his runny nose. Maureen, the newlywed, showing their matching gold rings, hovered around him, solicitous. The head of the hospital came to visit. Chuck's former secretary visited. His friends Dr. Don Weems and his wife, friends also of Maureen's, visited and met us. The woman minister who had married them visited.

We tried not to crowd him. All three sons came in and out. When others were visiting, or while the hospital staff changed his bedding, or treated him, we waited in a room down the hall.

While I was at his bedside, Judy called; another time Jack. His estate lawyer called also, long distance from Paris, France. The lawyer's wife had just died and he had gone to Europe for a break. His office had just found him. Chuck's sudden hospitalization had caught him unawares. Chuck put me on the line to speak with him, Jack Bernetich.

Bernetich rapidly explained the terms of the will that Chuck and he had finalized six months before, when Maureen had been designated as Chuck's fiancée. Certain properties and cash would go directly to Maureen; otherwise the bulk of assets–I had no idea of the figure until later, some 3.7 million–would go into a revocable trust. Chuck wanted Maureen "taken care of," by which he meant that he wanted her to continue in the life style they had shared. 55% of his estate would go into a trust for her, with the annual interest providing income. 45% would go into trusts of one third for each son. Bob, unless he had children, would be entitled to his share when he turned 40. Scott, as the most settled and reliable, would receive 34% of his third outright and 66% would go into trust for his children. Chuck Jr. as the derelict, whereabouts unknown, would get nothing; all would go to his children. The designation "fiancée" in the will now needed to be amended to "wife," and Chuck could now give Maureen $100,000 as a non-taxable gift. In addition to this, Bernetich wanted Chuck to reduce the estate by giving other non-taxable gifts while he was still alive. I had trouble following all this, even as I took notes, and Chuck would have to repeat it to me again later, when we were alone.

Also as Chuck's wife, Maureen wanted to be Chuck's executor instead of me, but Bernetich explained to her that she couldn't be. Eventually it was decided that Bernetich and I would be co-executors, instead of just me. All of this was tinged by emergency; that business must be concluded while Chuck was still alive and could sign things.

I didn't feel free to discuss the will with my nephews, who were anxious and talking amongst themselves in my hearing about something "not being right." Chuck said that Bernetich would send a copy to me later.

*

The sons had appeared, of course. They had been outside smoking as we first hurried in. Hugs, hellos. Later on, in a probate hearing, Bob would testify: "Apparently Maureen called my brother, Scott, and said your father and I got married; your father is dying; don't even bother coming, because he'll be dead before you get here. Then my brother called me. I ran down to the hospital." Even Chucky had been found and had flown in from out west. Each was seeking bedside reconciliation; each was hurting. But they were all upset at their father's sudden marriage and its implications on inheritance.

*

After the lawyer phone call, the phone rang again, and I answered it. "This is Nancy," the voice said, a voice I hadn't heard in over fifteen years. "Who's this? Dee? Can I speak to Chuck?"

I held the receiver: "Just a sec." Then I whispered to Chuck, "It's Nancy."

He made an emphatic, disgusted face, and waved me to hang up.

I felt awkward, not wishing to offend.

"He doesn't want to talk to you," I must have said. Or, "He can't talk right now. Do you want to talk to one of the boys?"

She said, no; but beyond that I don't remember her reply. I know it wasn't: "Tell him I love him," or "Tell him I'm sorry." Most likely, "Well, goodbye then."

*

Chuck and I had our private parting. He asked me one favor. When I got back to Boston, go to Newton City Hall and get a copy of his birth certificate from 1933 and Fedex it to Maureen to make the paperwork for his funeral easier.

We kissed, his stubble on my lips. My eyes welled. "I just don't like knowing I'll never see you again."

"It was a good life," he told me intently. "Love you, guy."

We returned to Boston. We called and got calls regularly from Maureen, from Judy, from Jack. The sons were still with Chuck, Maureen told us. The morphine levels he was taking were enough to kill him. He was hallucinating. He insisted on leaving the hospital to die in Maureen's new condo at one point; then would say no, the hospital was fine. He could be cared for better here. It would be easier on Maureen. She was ready to take him and everything they would need, the oxygen tanks, the medications, the hospital bed, but she was also alone. She confessed plaintively that she wouldn't know what to do. She was distraught.

*

Throughout the waiting, I thought of bodies, my brother's body lying in pietà posture in that hospital bed, as he slept snoring, lax, mouth agape, eyes closed, head back. Motionless.

We had a power failure in the heat wave. I lit a candle and drew a cold bath, soaking for twenty minutes and thinking about Chuck. But as I lay naked breathing, knees drawn up to my side in the shallow tub, the drain wouldn't close fully, so the twelve inches of water trickled gurgling through the rubber mat. I lay there, breathing, immersed, cooled by the water, candlelight flickering, thinking of Chuck's life ebbing like this, like the full tub of water, as he lay breathing. The energy, his life, gradually drained. The tub emptied, I sat up, twisted myself out.

Then Maureen called: he was gone.

The funeral was to be a memorial service at our family cemetery; his wish had been to be cremated and to have his ashes scattered on our plot, rather than to be buried there. The funeral director interviewed me long-distance for his obituary.

We drove down again, for the day, this time with Ruth and David along with us.

I was and was not my body, I thought, driving with my wife and children. My words were disembodied, my thoughts, my love. My lasting actions in this world. My physical presence had been beside the point of connection with my brothers and sister. We rarely if ever wrote words, just long-distance phone talk, vanishing utterance. Chuck's calls to me were usually drunken and misty with sentimentality. Now here I was on this visit to his memory, and dust. The car hurtled our seated bodies across distance. Writing notes for Chuck's obit, I had felt that I was saying nothing that mattered, that facts failed to portray him. I thought of Chuck as a surgeon, his life dedicated to healing bodies, serving bodies. I thought of his repeated confession to me that he felt frustrated at our parents' deaths, that his knowledge had proved powerless where love demanded most.

How could a cancer surgeon continue to chain-smoke and be caught unawares by a lung cancer so advanced as to be untreatable? And at age 65? When I saw him in the hospital Chuck had said he had more cancer than he had lung tissue.

It had not been diagnosed until, according to Don Weems, his friend, they had been out for dinner in January and Chuck had barely touched his steak. He'd been losing weight. Citing a 65-pound weight loss and respiratory problems, Don finally persuaded him to go for a check-up; they x-rayed his lungs and found the cancer, and immediately hospitalized him.

I can only surmise, but it seems likely that my brother knew he had cancer a good two years before it took him, and that this was the point when he had started sounding morbid on the phone and talking about his estate. It seemed likely that he chose not to be treated, not to fight it, which in Hazel's case he had called only "prolonging the dying." He didn't tell Maureen. I doubt that in those drunken phone calls he told anyone.

I spoke at the service, as did Maureen, and several of Chuck's doctor friends. None of his sons spoke. Afterwards we paid respects to the Henry family plot. At Mom's grave, I introduced Mom to Maureen.

For his two oldest sons, however, who left the funeral, found a lawyer the same day and filed a caveat against probating the will (as we discovered several weeks later), the true memorial was to be a lawsuit that would drag on for three years before being overruled. They contested the will, the marriage to Maureen, and invoked the divorce settlement from eighteen years before.

*

My role as staff at a summer writers' conference in California allowed me to combine visits to my sister with business. I had seen her, my nieces and grand-nephews several times in the years before Chuck died. I had also called Jack regularly, keeping up with his news and sharing mine, but I had not seen him since a business visit to Denver several years before.

Judy took the view that Chuck had sown the wind and reaped the whirlwind, at least in terms of family life. His values had created his marriage. His marriage had resulted in the neediness, misogyny, and despair of his children. She had no redeeming impression of Maureen, so she saw Chuck ending up with empty hands, wanting and needing love and faced with greed instead.

But what about the doctor, I wonder again, the healer, the contester with death? Didn't he know for himself, in himself, the rewards of helping others, even if they failed to love him back?

*

Chuck was a surgeon. Even his sons respected him for that, and tried to dedicate themselves in his shadow, as orderlies, as hospital staff in one capacity or another. He needed a studied, intuitive and long-experienced knowledge of disease and of the human body. He needed to read through symptoms to the hidden cause. If possible, I imagine he would have done his own laboratory tests; the whole technical apparatus and resource of medical specialties must have challenged his own sense of exactness and control. I need to think of him operating. I see the documentaries on TV of operations and I cringe, as an outsider, as I see the human body, without personality, anesthetized and inert as a slab of meat. There are the supporting nurses and doctors at hand. The incisions, the bloom of blood, the parting of muscle and fat, the clamping-off of arteries, the discovery of malignant tissue and its removal, the precise repair: these are actions not for pride, but for keeps. Nothing is trivial. Just as the surgeon can't forget the life and humanity of the flesh he cuts, he can't over-personalize it either. The rule against operating on your own kin, I think, must be founded on a principle of personal distraction. Under the knife, everybody is equal. No black or white, rich or poor, powerful or powerless; no ugly or beautiful; no beloved, no enemy. Every life is sacred.

He had his victories. Of course he also had his toll of losses. Offended by the way I had portrayed him in my writing, especially concerning his politics, he also let me know that he had a social conscience. That he often operated for free for patients who couldn't pay. That he had secretly put several poor kids through college. But that these things were private.

Those 300 operations in Africa must have satisfied Chuck, at least as a short-term gesture, and also must have worn against the grain of Maureen's expectations. She had assisted in some of them, but she was not a nurse. On a working vacation, after a point, she would have wanted them to enjoy themselves. Volunteering in Africa was not a way of life.

Why was Chuck drinking? Society itself had spun away from the world of the Eisenhower 1950s. Nothing had mattered to him more than the idea of family and yet his family had fallen apart in his hands. He had been betrayed. He had been exploited. And then his true gifts as a surgeon had been spurned. I think he turned himself against what he perceived to be society's ingratitude by turning against his own nature and the whole idea of service, and by swerving from what I saw as our mother's way to our father's.

I know that I feel frustrated myself, blessed in my marriage and children, and in my teaching, writing and editing, proud of differences I know that I make and have made; and yet disappointed that I haven't written the books that I felt meant to write, and that I haven't been more worthy as a human being. But I can't stop trying, as Chuck seemed to have stopped, and what my mother called "the great adventure of life" is fresh within me most mornings.

In his retirement Chuck didn't rediscover his talents for drawing or photography. His intense focus on building model ships, assembled from expensive kits, seemed to me a parody both of Mom's art in her final years and his own fine, fine, inspired control of a scalpel etching around living artery, vein and nerve. He must have elevated diversion into obsession. I don't know where he stood spiritually. He was a stoic and a skeptic, as I knew him. He had a bleak view of history, society, and the personal life. We come; we go. And yet Maureen said that he had told her that you could feel the passage of a soul with a dying patient, like a brush of wind past you.

I need to honor more freely his last words about his 65 years as a good life. I wish for his intimacy with Maureen, the "rare thing in this life when you can trust someone absolutely." I wish for her private, kindred depths; her true perception of his best self. I wish for the meaning of his money to him as love, as help to the living. I want to grant him his and Maureen's love on the order of mine and Connie's or of Jack's and Janice's. I want him to feel that his life was shared.

*

Judy, Jack and I did have our family reunion in Pasadena six weeks after Chuck's death. I had stopped in Los Angeles on my way to serve on the staff of a writing conference near Lake Tahoe, and Jack had arranged to fly out as well. I stayed in Judy's guest room and Jack at a nearby motel. We went to the Huntington Gardens to see the notorious "Corpse Flower," which only blooms once every century, looks like a four-foot-high phallus, and smells for miles around like rotting meat in order to attract the flies that pollinate it. Thousands of visitors had lined up wearing face masks to see the rare sight. What were we thinking? In any case, by the time we got there, the flower had been pollinated, the crowds were gone, and all we saw were the limp and deflated petals.

That evening we had a mock séance in Judy's living room; joking was our defense, as always. Here we are, Chuck. We summon you. Among these paintings and sculptures, John's, Judy's, Mom's.

One of our longstanding family pranks when we posed for pictures was to make a V sign behind each other's heads, like devil's horns. Judy kept a larger-than-life sculpture of John's that resembled Rodin's *The Thinker* in her storage room. She called it Big Foot. Big Foot was seated naked and brooding with astonishment at a bejeweled and multicolored skull held in his palm. I insisted that she take Jack and my picture together with it as we both gave Big Foot devil's horns, Death itself. John had died. Our brother had died. Our own turns would come, but here we are.

On Swimming

I was a good swimmer as a teenager, in a swimming family. My mother had been good and loved swimming still, even after operations in her shoulders and elbows for bursitis. She told stories about diving off cliffs at Cornell. My older brother Chuck was on the team at Martin's Dam and also at Haverford School. He swam a hard crawl and also butterfly and I don't remember if he ever won. My sister Judy, however, was more than good. She was a star on the Martin's Dam team, doing crawl, butterfly and backstroke, and practicing for hours in the lanes set up for fifty yards between the diving float and racing dock. At Baldwin School she swam races but also water ballet. She and her best friends, Kathleen and Cathy, practiced manically, and I went to their meets. I remember the smell of chlorine and slick seal-like clinging of wet suits, as well as the inane music of Blue Tango they used for ballet. For racing she specialized in racing dives and for backstroke in flip turns. I tried to imitate all this on my own, as a junior at our swim club, Martin's Dam. I don't remember if I ever placed. but I must have at some meet, second or third. We were given ribbons and badges. I remember the practices, grueling, under the aegis of the Martin's coach, Jules Provost, who was also my science teacher at the public school. I imitated Judy's water-ballet smoothness in my crawl stroke, turning my wrist to slide into the water, and cupping my hand for thrust, rather than slapping the water. When she swam, she seemed streamlined and effortless, gliding. She would pull ahead of her rivals so smoothly. Just the steady, powerful glide and pull, and she would surge ahead. I tried my best. But my wind, even after hours of practice, laps and laps, was never good for swimming. I could push myself to the brink of nausea, but that was never the equal of the gifted. I remember J.V. meets at Martin's. The shivery dawn. The butterflies in the stomach, which Judy had too and tried to calm with jelly beans. The pretense and pomp of a real race, team to team. Standing on the block, arms back, ready for a racing dive. The tense expectation of the starter's gun, then crack! And spring forward for a shallow splash and already churning kick, and stroke, pulling deep. My damnedest. Trying to keep in my lane. Barely aware of anyone ahead or behind. Plunging, digging each stroke, pull, kicking hard. Heart wild. Gasping every third stroke for breath. Harder. Hitting the slimy edge of the diving dock and ducking under for a tuck and turn, then push, glide, and back, pulling, digging, as my strength failed, arms ached, gasping, keeping in the lane, between the floats, kicking my best, can I make it, harder, one hundred yards, gasping, failing, and dimly aware of splashing in the adjacent lanes ahead of me, all body, all effort, finishing fourth, fifth, sixth, my hand hitting the dock. Heaving breath at the finish, hardly able to lift myself out. We had no swimming team, as Chuck did at Haverford, in school. This was only at the summer swimming club. Perhaps 9th and 10th grade. The meets were tense with other clubs, sometimes away. I remember Colonial Village, just down the street from Martin's. The different format, different pool. And shivering, having to show up early, early, Saturday at 8 a.m. When I got to college, swimming was too difficult a sport. Not only in muscle and stamina, but in time. At Amherst freshman year there seemed barely time to breathe and think, let alone go out for demanding sports, and swimming was one of the most demanding. I went to a couple of meets. I remember a star, Jack Quigley, now a doctor. The conditioning, the regimen, the dedication, and the performance were utterly beyond me. As for Chuck, I think he tried swimming at Franklin and Marshall, after he had flunked out of Cornell, but then he quit. Judy, I think, tried too at Swarthmore freshman year, but then she quit when she got pregnant and married an upperclassman. We never amounted to much, as swimmers. My mother, after our father died, lived alone in their suburban Philadelphia ranch house, and had the notion to install a swimming pool for health. In her late seventies, said she was too fragile to travel anymore, so she wanted to make her house a spa, where we all would visit. The pool, in a sheltered Plexiglas enclosure, became our baptismal pleasure, and we all clamored in, splashing, playing, with our wives and children. Alone, she swam laps for as long as she could. I don't swim much anymore, I confess. In my pre-retirement sixties, I am dedicated athletically to workouts in a gym. Neither my wife, my daughter, or my son are serious swimmers. Our New England waters are mainly Walden Pond (inland) or various beaches south of Boston and on the Cape, or the local MDC pool, less than a mile from our house. Walden for our family has spiritual connotations. From the time our children were young, we and friends would go there, stunned by the privacy no matter how crowded the park. Our family's best friends also swam there and had appropriated a beach near the original Thoreau cabin, on the far shore of the pond. Sometimes we joined them for picnics. Sometimes they went with our children and without us. My daughter, always precocious, sneaked into Walden as a teenager for illegal skinny dips. Years after these family friends had suffered untimely losses to cancer, first of their eight-year-old son (best friend to our son), and then of the father, Pat (a second father to our son), we rarely swam at all, and rarely took the trip together to a beach or to Walden. Now summers, in the heat, I may run ten or twelve miles around the Charles River, then dip in the MDC pool alone on the way back home. It is a shallow pool, crowded with frolicking teens and sub-teens, but exhausted and hot, it is a blessing on a long run. I try a few laps in the old free-style crawl of my sister, but my stamina is only good for twenty yards, if that. Sometimes, special times, my wife Connie joins me, and we swim together in these shallow, neighborhood waters. One of the lifeguards is Caitlin, sister and daughter of the family friends with losses to cancer. We are middle-aged. Two teachers. My wife at an elementary through sixth-grade school, to which she has given her life and now is assistant director, and me to Emerson College, where I have given my professional life. Two summers ago we are alone at Walden. We both feel the losses and the toll of time. But there is a lovely buoyancy. We wend our way through the paths around the rim of the pond and discover that our favorite spit has been reclaimed for conservation. We slip into the waters from a nearby beach. And the waters are warm. We swim together. The bottom falls away to the deep of the pond. I love my wife. I cannot speak to her or to others in words how much. She is a pure, constant and affirming soul against all the doubts and contradictions of living. My loving is not worthy of her. But in this twilight we swim as newlyweds.

The Guns in My Life

1. Boyhood Guns

I grew up in the 1940s in the shadow of my older brothers, Jack and Chuck, who were ages twelve and ten when I was born; my sister Judy was six and felt so oppressed by males that when I turned out to be a boy, she refused to look at me for several weeks. My brothers both went to Haverford School for Boys, where they were wrestlers, swimmers and baseball players. In our family movies they show off for the camera (with my father the cameraman), tossing a football or baseball. They were adventurers. They dug an underground clubhouse. They built a tree house.

During my first nine years, they had their own room across from mine, "the boys' room," where they accidentally exploded a chemistry-set alcohol lamp that they had filled with kerosene. They cast their own lead soldiers, with a kiln in which they melted the lead; then, with a lever, released it into a variety of different metal molds (for World War I tanks, artillery guns, machine-gunners, riflemen), which they then dipped into water and broke in half, releasing the shiny piece. They had an elaborate "O" gauge electric train set with tracks that went under and around their beds and out into the hallway and back. They were Boy Scouts, with sashes, and with knee-high boots that laced all the way up. Summers, they went to camp in the Maine woods, where they learned woodcraft, canoeing, and fly fishing. They tied their own flies. They jokingly rode saw "horses" in one family movie. In another they marched with BB rifles over their shoulders. For practice, they shot BBs out their bedroom room at crows on the branches of a tree in Captain Bones's yard (Bones himself, the Chief of Police, sometimes shot at the crows from his back porch with a .22 pistol).

When our uncle John came back from the Army, where he served in the Battle of the Bulge, he gave them a German gas mask in a fluted green canister with a swastika on top (they took turns wearing it for Halloween); he also had a captured 9mm Luger, which he once let Jack shoot. Dad himself had been 4F (thanks to his age and a bad leg) and served on the rationing board as well as being air-raid warden for our street. My grandparents had turned over their fifteen-room family house and furnishings in Wayne, Pa., as part of enticing my father home from Boston, where he had a career with Walter Baker Company, so that he could take over our family candy business, and so that my grandfather, who had heart problems, could retire. My grandparents then had leased a small nearby farm, where Jack had learned to shoot both my father's boyhood pump .22 squirrel rifle and a new .410 shotgun, a gift from my grandfather.

When we went to Saturday matinees, the newsreels were all about Allied victories: gritty, animated versions of news photos of Marines raising the flag, with baritone voice-overs. My favorite serials were Westerns, featuring such singing cowboys as Roy Rogers and Gene Autry, whose gun fights always had whining ricochets that I imitated with my friends in gun play ("pit-toooo!"). These and other cowboy heroes (Red Ryder, Tom Mix) were icons on kids' western outfits and belt-and-holster cap gun sets, and were featured in comic books and on the radio as well. There were also G-men "in peace and war" (with their automatic pistols, tommy guns, and snub-nosed revolvers) and such flying, caped superheroes as Captain Marvel or Superman, whose powers rendered guns irrelevant. One of my first toy guns had been a wooden tommy gun with a crank and clacker.

Jack told me later that his passion for guns and hunting predated my birth. My father's flamboyant sister, Peggy, had married a big-game hunter and playboy, Gail Borden, and during one visit by Mom and Dad, Gail had shown Jack his extensive gun collection, and let him help to clean them. After Gail and Peggy divorced, furniture and trappings from their house had found their way to our house, including one black bear rug and one polar bear, and two matching leopard skin rugs, each with marbles for eyes, ferocious mouths with ceramic teeth, and with real claws: apparently kills of Gail's.

In our home movies, there is a reel of me at Christmas in a sailor suit, and beside me sits Jack wearing a hunting hat, flaps down, and proudly cradling a new rifle, which must have been the .410 shotgun. Beside Uncle John's teaching him to shoot with this, Jack was influenced by a local gunsmith, Karl Roeder, who repaired a broken firing pin on the .410, and to whom Jack apprenticed himself for a time, casting and loading bullets, in return for two broken antique rifles, a muzzle-loading musket and a breech-loading Calvary rifle, one of the first to use a shell. Roeder and his wife had once belonged to a vaudeville shooting team, and Jack spoke of watching in awe as Roeder set matches in a bullet trap and lit them with pistol shots from across the room. By the time I was five, Jack had his driver's license and hunting license. He and his friends went hunting in the Poconos, where he shot a six-point buck with a slug. After they brought it home, Jack had its antlers mounted on a plaque and stored the meat in our grocer's locker, but when, as a family, we tried eating our first venison, none of us liked the "racy" taste and toughness.

We moved from the Wayne house to a smaller, but still roomy one in nearby St. Davids. I was turning eight. My brothers here had gabled rooms on the third floor, with their own bathroom between them. My own room was in back on the second floor, and had been a nursery. I shared a bathroom with my sister, whose room was just off the front stairs. In front was a guest room, and then the master bed room, each with private bathrooms. On the first floor besides the living room, sun porch, and dining room in front, was Dad's den, next to a lavatory, then the kitchen, and in back Mom's study and painting room, and a maid's bedroom, which Mom used as a sewing room. Dad's den had built-in bookcases, with glass doors. Jack appropriated this bookcase for a gun cabinet, building notches for rifle stocks on the bottom shelf and cutting notches for the barrels from an upper shelf. He also put in hooks for pistols.

By this time he had a double-barrel 12 gauge shotgun, the .410 shotgun, and over/under .22/.410, a bolt-action Garand-style .22 rifle with a clip and scope, the .22 squirrel rifle, and his prize, the Mannlicher-Schoenaur .308 carbine with scope, a deer-hunting rifle that he saved for and ordered from Germany; and four handguns: a Smith & Wesson .38 Snubby, a Smith & Wesson .357 magnum (for which he carved his own stocks, with a special thumb rest), an elaborate Ruger .22 target pistol, and an antique Colt ball-and-cap .44 with a six-chamber cylinder that he loaded from a powder horn, pushed in balls, tamped, and then fit with percussion caps. In the furnace and laundry room side of our basement (across from the finished playroom with a fireplace and bar), Jack installed a workbench, with a small lathe, and metal-working tools. He also had a foot-operated drill press. He made his own .22 pistol here from a cut-down rifle action. He melted lead in the old toy kiln and molded bullets; then loaded spent casings with primers and black powder, mainly .308 shells, but also .38s for the pistols. He kept tins of black powder the size of cookie jars on shelves in a closet alongside the massive oil furnace.

His primary passion was for cars, however. His best friends had been "grease monkeys" at Haverford. He had a Model A coupe at Bloomingdale, with a rumble seat. He also had a 1919 Cadillac touring car, which moved with us to St. Davids, and which he restored to the point that he drove it to Haverford, as well as to Eaglesmere, our summer resort. After flunking out of Cornell freshman semester, he worked for the local Buick dealership; he also rented a shop behind the dealership and opened a restoration business. The contacts he'd made by winning prizes for his Caddy at antique automobile shows provided more business than he could manage. He hired a friend to help, but decided to close the shop after two years.

These were Korean War years. He had joined a National Guard tank company, and during maneuvers had been hospitalized for asthma and told he was at high risk for TB. He was honorably discharged. The Army doctors advised him to live in the high, dry regions near the Rocky Mountains, so he enrolled in Colorado A&M, in Fort Collins, and left in his Ford coupe on Christmas day, 1951. Once there, he decided college wasn't for him, but he loved the West, which he called God's country. He worked in a lumber camp, driving trucks and clearing logging roads with a bulldozer.

In 1953, he hurt his back and was home again, in traction for six months in his third-floor room. There he read stacks and stacks of paperback Westerns (which I read later, and emulated in my first serious writing), and we played with my collection of plastic toy soldiers, tanks, and artillery on his rumpled covers. He'd be home two more years, during my early teens.

I prized my cap guns by how Jack commented on their realism. Imitation Peacemaker guns, resembling those in the cowboy serials, were chrome with white plastic grips; half the cylinder was a flap that opened, so you threaded a roll of caps inside and then clicked it shut. What was supposed to be the ejector rod was centered under the barrel, where it made no sense. They came in fake leather belt-and-holster sets, sometimes with loops for wooden or plastic bullets. My first Christmas at St. Davids, Mom and Dad gave me a set of genuine leather double holsters with a tooled belt—as good as Jack's—and a matched set of Peacemakers that had brass shells with aluminum bullets that pulled out (you loaded a single, circular cap inside the shell, refit the bullet, then loaded your six bullets into a solid cylinder that flipped out like those in Jack's Smith & Wessons); there was even a slide ejector slung off to the side that unloaded the shells, and each bullet had a hole drilled through, so that smoke from the fired cap came out the barrel. Jack was impressed. I had other, less favored guns as well: a detective special, a two-barrel pirate pistol, a derringer, and a small automatic, presumably a .32, with a pretend slot for where the spent shells kicked out. In imitation of Jack, I even built a gun rack from a hanging bookshelf in my room, cutting out slots for the guns to fit barrels down, in two rows.

Jack took me shooting for the first time when I was nine. His friend Buddy, more a hunting pal than a grease-monkey pal, owned a farm, and had set up a target range out back with bottles and cans. Jack had me fire his .22 carbine standing, sitting, and lying prone: deep breath in, let it out slowly, and steadily squeeze the trigger. I loved the report and slight recoil, the smell of cordite, and the shell kicking out as I worked the oiled bolt action, though I hardly ever hit anything. Jack himself was firing the Mannlicher-Schoenaur without ever missing, and then let Buddy try it. Bottles shattered, cans leapt and went flying. He had his ball-and-cap .44 as well, which went off with a roar, making my eyes wince, and the gun, Jack's hand and arm, all leap over his head. He laughed. "Son of a bitch, this thing's a cannon!"

Sternly, then and later, he lectured me in gun safety and morality. Whether a gun was loaded or not, you never pointed it at another person unless you meant to use it (a tenet that rendered all the more chilling his revelation to me years later that during the worst of Dad's alcoholism at Bloomingdale, Jack had leveled his loaded squirrel rifle at Dad and told him to leave Mom alone or he would shoot). More than for protection, guns were for hunting. Hunting was a test of prowess, tracking, knowledge of your quarry, and marksmanship for clean kills; you killed to eat, to skin, or to control population. You didn't kill for kicks.

My best friend from school, John Barnett, lived on a nearby dairy farm (his father was the tenant farmer and the farm was one of several owned by socialites who rode to hounds). We were in Cubs, and then Scouts together. We escalated from shooting cap guns from behind big rocks in the pasture or hay-bale forts in the barn loft to target shooting at cans with BB guns. At ten, I'd saved up and been allowed to buy a BB rifle: a plastic-stock, 50-shot pump repeater, with a special peep sight and a secret compartment where the stock met shoulder. John's BB gun was a Red Ryder 1000-shot model with a wooden stock and a trigger guard that you cocked. John's mother also supervised his shooting his father's .22 rifle in an effort to kill groundhogs in the pasture, whose burrows were hazards to the cattle. We would spot one sitting up at its burrow, perhaps 100 yards away (any closer and the groundhog dove back inside), and John would steady the rifle on the pasture gate, take aim, and fire. He never hit one when I was there—only a puff of dirt close by—but his father had killed one, and the survivor was its mate.

As I grew older, Jack lent me his .22 carbine to hunt rabbits, as well as groundhogs, with John. We always wore red, because there might be other hunters in the distant woods. For lack of quarry, and out of sight of the farm house (though cautious too about trajectories, and where bullets might end up), we shot at crows and squirrels. Once we exploded a grenade-sized glass jar that we had filled with powder from shotgun shells, using a string dipped in oil for a fuse. We were lucky not to get glass bits in our faces. John sometimes blew up frogs, shooting at point-blank range. My one kill was a rabbit, a sitting duck (as it were), in the middle of the bull pen, where we weren't supposed to shoot. Only five yards away, it wasn't a sporting kill, and when John opened the warm carcass with his knife, we found babies in its belly. It wasn't good for eating, he said; and feeling somehow ashamed, we hastily buried it.

Jack would have felt betrayed, and Mom and Dad alarmed, had they ever suspected me of playing with Jack's guns, but I found the temptation overwhelming. The cabinet wasn't locked. When nobody was home, I only hefted the pistols, at first, flipping open their empty cylinders, cocking the heavy hammers, un-cocking them. Peered down the rifled barrels. I may have opened a box of greasy .38 shells and slipped them into the chambers of the stubby, then clicked the cylinder shut, the way they did in realistic westerns. Then opened it again, and ejected all five shells smoothly at once. Later I would take the stubby and sneak around the house, pretending I was a detective, the real gun heavy in my grip. I'd make my shooting sounds, aiming down the well of banisters at pretend crooks or spies. The .357 magnum was too heavy and ungainly to play with. I was never tempted to fire the .38, inside or outside the house, but I did fire the .22 carbine.

There was a twenty-five-foot line of sight from the furnace through the opened door into the playroom to the playroom's deep stone fireplace. I could fire safely into logs there, or even into the blackened stone recess behind them without fear of ricochets. I loved the ear-ringing report of firing inside. I would only fire two or three times, then irresistibly, once more. I would run to make sure that I covered up the logs that had bullet holes, collected flattened slugs, and smudged any impact scars on the stone. Then I'd put away the little box of bullets, hide the spent shells in my pockets, and return the rifle to the cabinet. This all seemed harmless to me then. Looking back, I have to wonder why I hadn't been instructed more strictly, allowing for temptation, and why the cabinet wasn't locked; why the bullets weren't locked away; and even more, why Mom and Dad were so permissive towards Jack's passions, bizarre as they were in our suburban world.

Once his back was better (he had to wear a brace under his shirt), Jack went to Volkswagen mechanics' training, followed by a job with one of the first foreign-car dealerships, owned by a man who raced sports cars. Jack started hill racing. In our backyard, where the antique Caddy remained parked, he added three other cars: a boxy English Anglia, a Fiat sedan, and a Jupiter Javelin. He kept a welder and two acetylene tanks in our garage and worked with a cutting torch and protective mask, stripping the Anglia to its frame and cannibalizing the Fiat, in order to build his own hill climber, which looked like a buggy from Mad Max, with innards open to the air: gas tank, bucket seat, steering wheel, a roll bar, cables, wires, radiator, and the motor, which he had hopped up with a supercharger and modified valves. He won a few meets with it. Meanwhile he served as a pit mechanic in races for his boss; then got his Sports Car Club of America license, and drove his boss's racer at Sebring, Watkins Glen and elsewhere.

But this wasn't the life he wanted. He made an exploratory trip back west, with Chuck and me along for a brother-bonding, parent-funded adventure (I was 14, and we drove cross-country in his pickup and slept in a tent rigged in back), before making up his mind to settle in Ft. Collins and go into partnership in the excavating business. He took his guns with him.

Of course, I had my other passions. On my own, I had discovered sex and the mystery of women's bodies. Covertly, I studied paintings and photographs of nudes in my mother's *American Artist* magazines. I loved printing, beginning with toy presses and rubber type; then graduating to a hand-operated platen press and lead type (and eventually a mini-print shop that took over Jack's part of our basement). Influenced by Chuck, I loved photography, starting with box cameras and a toy darkroom set and moving on to 35 mm slides. When Chuck graduated from F&M in Lancaster, and left to serve in the Army in post-war Korea, he bought a Leica for himself in the PX and a Canon for me. I loved golf. I loved my Black Phantom Schwinn bike, which resembled a motorcycle. I loved our dog, Lady, whom Jack had brought back from Colorado and left with us. I read cowboy melodramas, mysteries, and sci-fi novels, as well as psychological classics that Judy and Mom urged on me. I loved writing, beginning with editorials for a newspaper I printed, to themes for school, to letters, to poetry, to the beginnings of a novel.

Just as Chuck left for the Army, Judy got married (her husband had been a senior at Swarthmore, and she dropped out at the end of her freshman year and settled in Harrisburg). As we visited Judy, I became the family photographer: first of her pregnancy, and then of my nephew's infancy (I was an uncle, I boasted to my 15-year-old friends). A year later, Jack got me work on a ranch in the mountains. I stayed with him in his Ft. Collins trailer for a few days before he drove me up. I photographed his equipment: a drag-line crane, bulldozers, dump trucks, and several backhoes, all painted white and blue with a prominent "Devers/Henry Excavating" logos; I photographed him digging a basement with his backhoe. I tried to document his life for our parents. I also tried to document my four weeks working and living with itinerant hay hands, an experience closer to Steinbeck's "Of Mice and Men" than to anything in Luke Short.

I returned the following year; and the year after that, after my high school graduation, we all drove out together for Jack's wedding; and although Chuck was just back from Korea, I was the wedding photographer. The bride, June, was a divorced mountain woman, two years older than Jack; she had three young children, and she shared Jack's love of guns, hunting, and fishing. They went on family hunting trips into the mountains. Thanks to Dad, Jack was able to buy out his partner and to build a new house, which also served as the office, shop, and shop-yard for the growing company.

I left home for Amherst College that fall. Despite my boyhood fascination with guns, I became neither shooter nor hunter. I became a writer, an editor, and a teacher, and settled in Boston.

2. Parenting My Son

My only gun now is a repeating air pistol from Daisy, outlawed in Massachusetts. I bought it during the summer that my mother was dying, and she was kept awake by squirrels throwing acorns from the tree outside her bedroom. Even then, in 1984, air guns had been outlawed in Delaware Country, Pennsylvania, where she lived, and I had had to drive to Lancaster to buy the pistol.

To discourage the squirrels, I first had tried hurling back the nuts, then a slingshot: to no avail. But the BB pistol surprised them. I stung one or two, and they chirred in rage. Others I scared as the BBs ripped nearby leaves, or hit nearby twigs. When Jack visited from Colorado, and Chuck from New Jersey, they each took turns shooting—at least until the neighbors complained—but the squirrels finally retreated, and Mom was amused by our regressions to boyhood.

Chuck had married a nursing student while I was in college, and had three boys over the next four years as he finished his internship and took a residency in Woodbury, New Jersey (his boys never pursued gunplay that I recall, but instead immersed themselves in Dungeons and Dragons). As for me, I went from college to graduate school, where eventually I met Connie, a Head Start teacher. We married in 1973; moved from Cambridge to Watertown, and had my daughter Ruth in 1977, and adopted my son David as an infant from Korea in 1985.

Before David's arrival, and after several years of getting by on grants for my writing and for the literary magazine I had co-founded, we were each hired full-time: me at Emerson College, and Connie at a private elementary school. Our closet family friends were anti-war activists, the Farrens, whose oldest daughter was my daughter's best friend, and who, just as we adopted David, had a son, who became his best friend, Gabe. On principle, the Farrens banned guns for Gabe, and Connie followed suit with David, although somehow plastic swords, arrows with suction cups, and rubber hatchets and knives were tolerable. Water guns and super-soakers, however, were more difficult concessions.

I found such thinking specious and blind to the nature of boys, especially such active boys as Dave and Gabe, who by age three had already been fashioning guns from blocks or fingers. Besides which, cowboy play seemed relatively innocent, emphasizing skill (fast draw, straight-shooting), honor, and justice; the sheriff or the lone hero fought evil and protected the weak, much as knights of old. True, this romance, as well as the romance of just war, had been tarnished for members of the Vietnam War generation, and even I had been put off by another of Dave's playmates (whose dad had served in the National Guard), showing up at our house in combat fatigues with a collection of the latest G.I. Joe figures.

Nevertheless, on a return trip home from Indiana, where I had spoken at my first writers' conference, I couldn't resist the perfect set of two-guns, belt, holsters, badge, and cowboy hat that I spied in the airport gift shop. "Oh, no, you didn't!" Connie protested, but once she saw Dave's face light up, she granted us the male prerogative. We have pictures of the occasion: Dave at three-and-a-half poses hat pulled low, standing in his blue bootie pajamas, holsters on both hips and six-shooters brandished at the camera.

Cowboy play took over. Dave agreed to put away the holster set when Gabe was over, but otherwise they played at being unarmed cowpokes, both dressed up in big hats and bandannas, and even chaps, and whooped it up side by side as they rode chaise lounge mattresses, with ropes as reins, which held up the front ends like horses' heads.

Dave bragged to Gabe that I had been a real cowboy, and showed him the picture of me on horseback at the ranch at age 16, which Connie had framed.

While Pat took Gabe and Dave fishing together, played basketball and baseball with them, and took them swimming, I was never as generous with Gabe as Pat was with Dave. On the contrary, I was jealous of my time alone with Dave, watching TV, mowing the grass, playing on the playground, or going on bike hikes. Before Dave's arrival, I had moved *Ploughshares* into a nearby storefront, and continued to work there when I wasn't teaching. It was a boxcar-length 1200 square feet (first floor and basement). When Dave went there with me, I set up a shooting range, using a chair back to shoot from at one end, and a big open carton and cardboard flaps at the other, where I tacked cartoon targets that I drew. I kept the BB pistol in my desk and ceremoniously showed Dave how to hold it, aim, release the safety, and shoot, despite how heavy and unwieldy it was for him. We took our peppered targets proudly home to Connie, who trusted me to be safe.

Gabe was diagnosed with liver cancer when he was seven, and for the next year and a half, he underwent a liver transplant; more cancer, then chemo; then strokes after the cancer metastasized to his brain. He remained plucky throughout, and Dave as his playmate kept by his side, both believing that he would get well. They had gone to Disneyland together (compliments of the Make-a-Wish Foundation); on a trip to Boston's Chinatown, where Gabe's mom had bought them matching white karate outfits, Chinese masks, and rubber nunchuks (inspired by *Power Rangers* and *Mutant Ninja Turtles*). In my last memory of Gabe, he lies in a hospital bed in the Farrens' living room, with Dave on the bed beside him. They are allowed to watch their first R-rated movies on TV and to fire realistic toy carbines at the villains and monsters there. Gabe died just before his ninth birthday; and the loss burned deep into Dave's psyche, compounded by the loss of Pat, "his second father," four years later, also to cancer.

From Connie's school, Dave went on to a private middle- and high-school at Beaver Country Day. Meanwhile, Ruth left home for college at Hampshire, and he moved into her downstairs bedroom. He made new, fast friends, primarily through sports (basketball, soccer, and baseball, all of which he played with talent and passion), but otherwise complained of being bored. Putting off homework to the last second, he spent hours watching ESPN, *The Simpsons,* and *South Park.* He hated school. He hated going to bed and hated getting up. He challenged and resisted the whole skein of adult life. His room was private, with a chain lock. Minor irritations over food, clothes, cleaning his room, or watching TV would escalate to door-slamming rages. I had bought him a home gym machine for his room, and he would try to work off his anger by weight lifting, hip hop blaring. We gave him his own PC with internet access, which he used for downloading and playing music, for games, for instant messaging, and probably for porn (which I discovered on the machine later, and he said must have been downloaded by his friends). However, we refused to let him have his own TV, since he was clearly addicted.

Of the cap guns I gave him over time, his favorite looked like a black 9 mm Glock. It broke open to reveal an eight-cap cylinder, which you fit with a plastic wheel of caps (I would get these from the corner grocer). The caps were too loud, so Connie had banned them from the house; still, he and his friends would lie around his room, clicking away at the ceiling. If guns were still in his imagination—and they did seem to recede in favor of sports, video games, sex, and love (symbolized by wall-sized posters of Britney Spears and Magic Johnson)—they were gangsta guns. Where "hood" lifestyles had been subversive in my adolescence, epitomized by Elvis and Marlon Brando, the teen fad now was for the drug and protest culture of rasta (Dave wrote a paper on Bob Marley and later added his poster to his wall) and hip hop. The heroes of this music, which Dave insisted on playing up high, as we car-pooled to and from school, and kept as a soundtrack constant in his room, were lowlives in the high life, often boasting about the "bitches" they raped, the rivals they shot, the drugs they scored, and the money they made. Their dress, adapted to teen consumers, were gold chains, high-priced knockoffs of Goodwill hand-me-downs: sports sneakers, oversized jeans with cuffs underfoot and waists slipped under their butts, exposing boxer underwear, outsized jerseys, and baseball caps (preferably worn backwards).

Dave was ironic and funny, as were his white suburban pals. So as they chanted along with the songs, or dressed in imitation ghetto, I thought they were making fun of the fad; the same with sex talk, drug talk, and with violence on TV. Dave himself said that they were sophisticates, taking none of this seriously. But clearly the appeal went deeper. As I objected to the lyrics, he tried to enlighten me about the artistry, the oppression and poverty overcome, and the real life success stories of performers such as Snoop Doggy Dog, Puff Daddy, or Tupac Shakur; and how they hired their extended families as they became rich. He saw it as the rebel's path to success.

I took this gang-banger mythology as a perverse substitute for the gunslinger fantasies of my boyhood. Interestingly, Dave's first introduction to literary tragedy was the Baz Luhrmann film *Romeo + Juliet,* where totemic gang guns replaced swords in a feud between drug lords. Connie and I worried about all this, and about how pop culture fed Dave's frustrations and anger. My own theory was that his anger was rooted in grief, over Gabe, over adoption, over difference, and over Ruth's absence, all combined with peer pressures against our life style and values. He also longed for power over his own body and life. Given the cultural surround of environmental doom, political oppression, terrorism, AIDS, and divorce, he despaired of the future and sought instant gratification from life, as if it were TV. His closest friends, he said, were all ADD, and refused to take Ritalin. My own, or indeed Jack's rites of passage, were no index to his.

Most of his meltdowns were directed at Connie, as Mom, the very person to whom he was most attached. At 13, when she tried to limit his TV time: "No wonder Ruth left! I'm leaving this house as soon as I can!" At 14, cursing, hacking the new kitchen counter, throwing Connie's flowers, and berating me as I try to stop him: "What're you going to do, call the police? You hide in the basement. You don't care or know anything about me! I hate you guys!" Or over something, else, locked in his room, and breaking prized possessions in order to hurt us by spiting himself: "Don't you ever tell me what I think or feel. You don't know!" At 15, he flatly refused to go to school one day, triggered by Connie's nagging him about helping with a diversity speech for her school. At 16, to me: "You live in a cave in your cellar! Go back down! You can't even name ten of my friends. You aren't interested in my life!"

My male example, he saw as flawed and weak. To him, I was always in my basement study, preoccupied with writing and reading. I was tight-fisted and cheap. I defied consumer culture. I couldn't choose presents to please Connie. I drove junk cars, which embarrassed him in front of friends. I always looked for bargains and refused to invest in quality. I wasn't wise. I couldn't fend off death. I didn't know how to control his rages and explosions. His models were elsewhere: in memory, the attentive Pat; at Beaver, the intimidating Mr. Manning, in charge of discipline; or among others, his pal Jay's flashy and divorced, permissive Dad.

He never blew up in public, at school, or as a guest elsewhere; the tantrums were reserved for us. We did our best to cope, and to help. On the one hand, he was the Dave we thought we knew: cheerful, sociable (so much so that teachers blamed him for distracting classes with his "socializing"); the generous, loyal pal, with his tribe of friends, including girls, brooding over their struggles and sharing his own with them; the charmer; the comedian; the sports, music, gaming, and movie maven; the clothes tree; the workout athlete, who spent hours on his machine, sweating himself up, consuming protein drinks and developing powerful arms, shoulders and chest; the sprinter; the prankster; the clever negotiator. On the other hand, he was easily frustrated. He refused to accept blame. "I always had a temper, even when I was a baby," he told us. He saw Connie's determined effort to have him face consequences as beside the point. When there were explosions, they were our fault, for not heeding his warning signals.

Together and separately we agonized. We were afraid of the depth of his anger, which was irrational, and which we feared would mar his life later. He also badly wanted his driver's license and we worried about his acting out as a driver, endangering himself and others. We tried to make him take responsibility for his meltdowns; to clean up; to pay with his allowance; to be grounded or denied TV. At the same time, guided by self-help books, we tried to treat his "chronic inflexibility" more as constitutional than moral. We tried to avoid the triggers. Offensive language, and even his incessant music we could live with; damage to property or to himself, we had to make a stand about. Everything in between was negotiable, such as household rules. We also insisted that he start professional teen counseling, which would be paid for by our health plan. He balked at and fought the notion, even demanded that we pay him for going, but he did go; and after several sessions, which he complained were a waste of time and money, he announced that he had the plan for another tattoo (over my objections, and despite the state law against tattooing minors, the first had been for his sixteenth birthday; with Connie's permission, he and Ruth had gone to the house of Ruth's friend who worked in a tattoo parlor, and Dave had gotten the Korean figure for "sister" and Ruth the one for "brother" tattooed on their respective backs). Again I cautioned: don't do something impulsive that your adult self might regret later. But he was excited, and when he showed us the design: "RIP Gabe/Nov 17/RIP Pat," we recognized it as the first serious articulation of his grief. A few weeks later, when Connie took him to a parlor, they refused to bend the law. He would have to wait.

3. Goodbye, My Brother

Guns had their role in my saying goodbye to Jack, and in Jack's attempt to pass on their mantle of power and manhood to Dave.

Dave's fourteenth summer had seen both my brother Chuck's untimely death (a divorced cancer surgeon, he had died from lung cancer, which he had known about without telling us), a trip for Dave and Connie to sightsee the Grand Canyon and Sante Fe, and then in August, my reunion with Judy and Jack in Los Angeles. A writers' conference had paid my way to California; Judy lived there, long divorced herself and near her daughters and grandchildren; and Jack flew in from Denver to join us. Over the years, our visits to each other had been infrequent, and the only times we'd all been together had been for our parents' funerals. Our love ran deep, however; and we normally kept up several times a year by phone. We missed Chuck. We wondered which of us would be missing next.

Jack was in good health, I thought, except for his asthma, and still hopeful in work and happy in his second marriage.

June had divorced him twenty years before. He had adopted and raised her children and built up his excavating business, but as his sons had come of age, the hard-drinking, brawling, and woman-chasing culture of working class Ft. Collins had claimed them. They'd married early, had children, and divorced; they were in trouble with the courts. Jack felt that he had lost them both, and that only his daughter appreciated him. June herself had mental problems. She flew with him in the 1939 Grumman staggerwing airplane that he had restored, used for work, and took to meets. She tried to run the office. But when he invented and built a massive pipe-laying machine, which he called the straddler, and there was promise of his selling the patent for big money, something in her had snapped. He spoke of her raving naked outside the house and waving a pistol. In the settlement, he kept his machine and his airplane, while June took the house and the money from the liquidated business. He moved to Pierce, twenty miles east of Ft. Collins, and started over, marrying Janice, who worked in the county sheriff's office, and who also had been divorced, with grown children. An economic downturn killed any hope of selling his patent, so he set out to manufacture two straddlers each year on his own. His plane allowed him to visit far-off sites, do maintenance, and make sales.

I had visited him in Pierce in early 1990, this time after attending a writers' convention in Denver, and he had shown me around his new life. He and Jan had a small ranch house with a garage in back, and a kitchen picture window that overlooked the distant mountains. I had met Jan years before, when they had visited us in Boston. She was younger than Jack, intelligent, attractive, cultivated, and more his natural partner than June. I stayed in their basement guest room. Pierce was a crossroads, population 800 or so, with one paved thoroughfare, a grain elevator, a water tank, a post office, a train depot, a grocery store, and several small businesses that served the surrounding farms, one of which was a lunchroom called "Load N' Chute," where Jack took me for breakfast and introduced me to the lazy-speaking morning regulars, mostly farmers. Then he took me down the main road to a sizable factory building and its two or three acres of baked gravel at the town's outskirts. On the building's front, foot-high letters spelled out "Henry Machine Co," and in front was parked Jack's masterpiece, a newly completed "Henry Pipe Layer," painted bright orange.

Overall, the machine was as wide as a locomotive is long; it traveled forward in its width on two caterpillar tracks, normally separated by 30 feet across, with lateral sections (engineered for stress) that could double its span. On one side was the glass-enclosed operator's cab with seat and controls; in the center was a hydraulic crane that swiveled, flexed, and extended; and on the far side a hopper for gravel, which could be replaced by a crib for holding sections of pipe. There was also a conveyer belt, which swung out to distribute gravel from the hopper. A powerful diesel motor was situated underneath the cab and crane assembly. Laying pipe of different sizes usually involved several different machines, highly paid operators, and a sizable crew (a backhoe or trenching machine for digging, a crane to lift and settle the sections of pipe, and a bulldozer for backfill, not to mention dump trucks and flatbeds) and only progressed a hundred feet a day, if that; but Jack's machine, as an all-in-one, could lay eight-hundred feet a day with a smaller crew, and thereby pay for itself. It sold for over a million dollars, and cost Jack perhaps half that amount to produce and service. The sale of one machine capitalized production of the next, and an unsold machine, including the one in his lot, cost Jack money unless he could lease it out. So far, he had sold five straddlers, which were actively working big jobs in Arizona, Montana, Illinois, Oregon, Calgary (Canada), and elsewhere. The one in Montana was laying pipe in the mountains, and Jack spoke proudly of its ability to operate on steep, side-hill terrain.

Orders had been falling off, however. He'd been working on a dream deal with the government of Iraq for a whole fleet of machines, but Washington had interfered, and in the meantime, his 1982 patent was running out. To keep his factory and crew of five busy, he'd begun producing carnival trailers—hydraulically powered amusement rides that folded up into drivable semis. It was steady, unchallenging work. Inside the building were cranes, chains, cutting torches, welding tables, stamping presses, drill presses, and other heavy equipment that allowed him to cut, bend, mold, and shape steel as if it were plastic.

Next day, we drove to Ft. Collins, where his plane was stored in a hanger, and he took me up for several hours' flight over vistas of whitened peaks, stretching west. We spoke through earphones and breathed oxygen, slowly clearing and circling the 14,255-foot Long's Peak, among others. We flew over Grand Lake. Everything, except for trees or barren stretches of rock, was covered in snow. We flew to North Park, a sea of white, and along the western range, Jack pointed down. He was circling the ranch where I had worked at age 16 and had written about in college. I recognized it from the air, though it was now blanketed in snow: main house, outlying bunk house, shop, barn and corral, the winding creek; I felt as though we were traveling in vastnesses of time as well as of space.

Even before our Los Angeles reunion, he'd been forced to sell the plane. Shortly after the reunion, his business problems worsened. He lost the lease on his big building and had to relocate to a garage near the center of Pierce, letting three men go. Along with the last straddler, he sold his patent to the Montana contractor, all to pay off a big bank note. He was still doing carnival trailer work, but when snow collapsed the garage roof, there wasn't insurance; he auctioned off everything and retired. At the same time, his health declined. In 2000, he was hospitalized for eight days with an "acute exacerbation" of Chronic Obstructive Pulmonary Disease. Earlier attacks had sent him to emergency rooms and run up bills for x-rays. He had stopped smoking and occasionally needed oxygen, but now specialists put him on a steady regimen of oxygen, antibiotics, steroids, and other medicines. For stretches the steroids would help, but they also damaged his immune system, and after a bout of pneumonia, which had begun with a cold caught from his grandchildren, and which had nearly killed him, he resisted taking them. He couldn't trust the doctors. He couldn't travel. He couldn't leave his house, except for short periods of time. Friends had to come to him. He needed oxygen all the time. On waking, he would spend hours just clearing his clogged lungs. Jan was loving, always, and together they took the challenge of his disease and fought it, hoping to find a way of slowing its progress and keeping quality of life.

The more I heard about his illness (just hints at first, in occasional phone calls and emails, which were cheerful mostly, in the spirit of coping), the more I worried how much time he had left. Despite the distance, cost, and my teaching duties, I felt that I had to see him. I kept him up on our news—Dave's getting his driver's license, Connie's teaching and mine, my struggle with department politics, Ruth's travels to Cuba, Italy, and Israel, her art projects with homeless teens, and her Fulbright grant to Colombia. I sent him pictures, and my writing; I shared my anxiety about my elevated PSA: all in an effort to stay close. I didn't want him to withdraw the way Chuck had. Judy worried too. I couldn't imagine such an active man being cooped up and helpless like that. Above all, I wanted David to meet him while he could. Connie had to work, but she urged me to go and take David with me. So in July of 2002, we set off on our first trip together, father and son: flying to Denver, renting a car, driving to Ft. Collins and checking into a motel, all of which I had arranged on the computer. Jan had warned us that they couldn't put us up.

*

Dave loved traveling. His trip with Connie earlier to the Grand Canyon had been an adventure. He was seventeen now and heading into senior year. He had no memory of meeting Jack as a four-year-old, or of going up with Ruth, Connie, and me for a ride in the staggerwing, where Jack had let Ruth steer, or of posing for a snapshot in his pajamas between Jack in his red jumpsuit and me in my T-shirt and running shorts, we three men on the porch steps, smoking chocolate cigars. I had been teaching in Iowa City that summer, and Connie had driven out with Ruth and David to join me. Jack had flown in from one of his business trips for the weekend.

Dave had only heard cursory stories, otherwise. After I had brought back pictures of Jack's factory, he fantasized about Jack's building him a motorized go-cart. We'd never really asked, of course; for fear of costs, shipping problems, local laws, and our lack of anywhere to ride it safely. But for several years, at any mention of Jack's name, Dave wanted to know when we would ask.

Now, on our flight to Denver, Dave retreated between earphones or slept. Once we landed, he wanted to drive the rental car, but finally accepted the rule that drivers be over 21 and put up with my driving and confusion about routes. As soon as we reached Ft. Collins and got settled, I called Jack, and Janice answered. She said he was sleeping and tomorrow would be fine to visit, but to call first, around noon. Next morning, Dave struggled to get up by 11 (at home, he kept a vampire schedule, up all night watching TV, or instant messaging, if not out with friends, then sleeping late, which I saw as his way of avoiding us). I went for a run along the highway outside, and was impressed when I came back to find him dressed, watching TV and ready for lunch. We drove around Ft. Collins a little. Bluish, snowcapped mountains lined the horizon to the west, with foothills starting just outside the city limits. I thought I knew the streets, but now the city seemed strange, having tripled in size. Colorado State University went on for blocks and blocks, surrounded by boutiques, bookstores, and exotic restaurants, as well as by the usual franchises and malls. We had our Wendy's. This time when I called, Jack answered. I wanted Dave to see the Rockies, so our plan was first to drive down to Loveland, up through Estes Park and onto Trail Ridge Road ("the highest continuous paved road in the world"); then return and arrive at Jack's for dinner. "Come on," he said.

The mountains were majestic. For Dave they rivaled the vast chasm of the Grand Canyon, but upside down, crowding the sky. The road climbed to 12,000 feet, well past the tree line and tundra. As a teenager, I had mocked my own father's timid driving on this road when our family first visited and toured. Now as the driver myself, I cringed from sheer drops without guard rails. We were eye-level with opposing peaks, and the intervening valleys spread thousands of feet below. I knew we'd need time to get back, so I stopped just before the highest point to turn around. But Dave insisted on getting out to explore first, marveling at the snow stakes as high as telephone poles, then climbing the slope up from the road to pose on rocks. I felt unsteady, but climbed after him. We took each other's pictures.

The distances, the amplitudes, the alpine breeze and vivid sky, still lingered in our senses, as we drove back to Ft. Collins. From there we followed Jack's directions East, passing large stockyard feeding pens along the way; also alfalfa and beet fields, with elaborate ranks of sprinklers that cast their intersecting arcs. Dave with his beagle nose was overwhelmed by the smells, mainly of manure.

I tried to spark his interest in meeting Jack. "He's funny," I said. "He's a great story teller. He was like a dad for me, growing up. He's a genius mechanic—Hey, mind if I turn it down for a minute? Okay.— All his life, he's loved cars." Dave stared out at the fields. "He restored antique cars. He drove racing cars. He even came in third behind Sterling Moss once." Dave turned: "Who's that?" "Moss? One of the all-time greats back in the sixties, sort of like Dale Earnhardt now." I explained about Jack's coming to Colorado for his asthma, then dropping out of CSU and starting up his excavating business. "We also took some road trips out here, too, Jack, Chuck and me together, with me the little brother. They both loved fly fishing, and I didn't. I didn't like the little bones in the trout they caught. I was your age when Jack got me the job on the ranch. Remember the picture? Me on the horse?" "Yeah, I thought you were doing round-ups and stuff." "No, just a hay hand, for the hay harvest. They let me drive a scatter rake pulled by a little Jeep tractor. That's how I got the nickname, 'Ol' Speed,' or 'Speedy.' You and your buddies could probably get work up there next summer, if you wanted." "Yeah, thanks, no thanks." In bits and snatches, I told him again about the airplane and the straddler, but what caught his attention most were the guns. "He's got a whole collection of guns, shotguns, deer rifles, and pistols; even a .44 Magnum like Dirty Harry's." "Can we see them? Think he'll let us see them?" "Sure," I said, "let's ask. But we'll have to play it by ear, okay? He's really sick, remember."

Entering Pierce, I recognized the water tower, the grain elevator, the railroad depot, and stores. I turned down Main Street, and around to Jack's gravel street, passing houses on both sides, and pulled up in front of his house, a car and pickup in the driveway. Jan greeted us at the door; and as Dave followed me inside, Jack stood smiling in the kitchen doorway, with his oxygen clip under his nose and the plastic tubing trailing behind him. We each hugged Jan hello, but Jack apologized for being unable to touch or hug us because of his immune system; germs could kill him (Jan was okay because they lived together, but anyone from outside could give him something). I was proud to present Dave. "My god, look at this guy," Jack said. "You're all growed up!" He shook his head. Off to one side, a contraption that looked like a dry vac hissed away, with its lengths of plastic tubing that coiled and led to Jack. "That's Jack's oxygen pump," Jan said. "He didn't like the way it worked, so he tinkered and modified it; it changes the air to oxygen, so he's got a constant supply." "Like fish gills, neat," I said. "Yeah, something like that," Jack said. "God, it's good to see you. Come on into the kitchen, let's sit down."

We had arrived for dinner. We sat at the dinner table while Jan cooked. Jack sat at the head with the back door open, providing circulation so he wouldn't pick up germs, and Dave and I sat a few seats down. We spoke about his finding a specialist he could trust. He showed us a clamp that fit on his finger and monitored his blood oxygen level. The oxygen tether was long enough to follow him through the house. He and Jan were hopeful about folk remedies that they had researched on the computer, especially colloidal silver, which sounded far-fetched to me; but Jack had ordered a jar and took some orally every day. Jan explained that it killed different microorganisms, especially staph.

Dinner was ready. She brought us plates and bowls. Soup, steak, baked potatoes, beans, corn on the cob: all delicious. She sat near Jack. But as we ate, Jack barely touched his full plate. He had no appetite, he said. And Jan: You have to try. A few more bites, hon. Please.

"I've been admiring your rogues' gallery there." I pointed at the framed photographs that filled the wall behind Dave: Grandpop Thralls as a young man, Nana Thralls in a bustle, pictures of Mom, her two brothers and sister, Dad and Mom, Chuck, Judy, me, a formal portrait of Grandpop Henry. I was touched by the display, particularly by several tintypes that I hadn't seen before (passed on apparently by Mom to Jack after her mother's death). Dave turned to look. "Yes, we're very proud of that," Jan said. "I love researching genealogy." Her own parents and children were there as well.

Jack and I started trading family stories for Jan's and Dave's benefit, and Dave was rapt. In connection with Dave's getting his driver's license, Jack told about when he had been fourteen or fifteen. "I kept bugging Dad to let me drive, but he said no. So one day, when he was away, I went up into the attic in Bloomingdale, where there were all these old trunks. You know, those big steamer trunks of Nana's and Aunt Peggy's? Anyhow, I found Nana's old clothes. I put on a fancy, oversized dress—Nana was big—and a big old hat with a veil. I figured the veil made up for not having a wig." I laughed; I'd never heard this. "So I go down, get in and start the car. I'd never driven before, just back and forth in the drive. I back out onto Lenore Avenue. I start to get the feel for the clutch. I'm into first, and second. I turn onto Bloomingdale. I'm having a fine old time. Stop, start. I drive down past the school, but suddenly I see a cop car following me. There's that hill up to the pike, and on the way up, I stall out. I can't get it started again. The cop car stops. And who gets out, but Captain Bones. 'Excuse me, ma'am, is something wrong?' He's our next door neighbor and Chief of Police. He'd spotted me and followed me around the block. 'Can you take your hat off for me, please, ma'am?' Of course, they took me to the station. They impounded the car. Dad had to go get it later. They called Mom, 'We've got your boy here, driving without a license and dressed up like a woman!' I got off with a warning. Meanwhile Dad was too tickled by the whole thing to be mad for long." We laughed together until we wept.

"I love these stories," Jan said. "Remember when Chuck was here? You two were up all night."

"You guys, how did you get away with it?" I asked, thinking of Dave's escapades with his friends, their freedom on the web, their overnight parties, their experimenting with sex and drugs, and overall their defiance of authority. "Chuck plays with matches and sets a closet on fire. You all keep deviling the elevator man in the apartments on the corner. You blow up chemistry sets. You sneak out at night. You shoot out your back window at crows."

"Who says we got away with anything? Dad was always ready with his razor strap. Remember the time Chuck tried padding his pants with comic books, but forgot to cry; and Dad kept whaling away harder and harder and couldn't figure what was wrong; then when he finally figured it out, he gave it to him for real? But seriously, nothing we did was ever meanness. Just boy stuff. Besides, Dad sort of half-sympathized, after he'd been held down by Nana; and Mom had grown up with three brothers. But how about you, little brother?"

"Me? I was tame compared to you guys."

"What about your printing? You printed up that bunch of Christmas cards that said, 'Merry Commercial Holiday from an Agnostic.'"

Dave laughed. He was loving this, listening to every word.

"Say, here's a question," I said. "You still have your guns?"

"Sure I do, yeah. Why do you ask?"

"Dave was hoping he could see them. He's never seen or handled a real gun. And I was telling him about the handguns."

"Well, sure.—Help me, hon." He and Jan got up. He started through the kitchen and down the hall, dragging the tubing behind him. Jan followed. They returned, each carrying two pistols—three in shaped holsters, one in a red silk bag. Jack settled back in his chair, and pulled out the .357 Magnum, which I recognized, with its oiled bluing, and the special wooden grip with the thumb rest. He passed it over to me. It felt like three pounds, with its six-inch barrel. I opened and closed the cylinder, and passed it carefully to Dave, butt end first. "That one's the cannon," Jack said.

"What happened to the .44?"

"I sold that years ago. That thing was a monster."

Dave held the .357 in both hands and sighted away from us. "Did you ever shoot this one, Dad?"

"Yeah, a few times, long time ago. I remember we were shooting at rats in the Ft. Collins dump. The recoil from it practically knocked me over."

"I don't like shooting that one, either," said Jan. "It's too much gun."

"Wow, it's heavy!"

Jack passed around the familiar .38 snubby, as well, and then a new Taurus .22, a beautifully balanced eight-shot with a six-inch barrel. Then he opened the red bag and pulled out a nickel plated .32, not much bigger than the snubby. "This was Grandpop Thralls's."

"So this is it!" I'd heard about, but never seen the pistol that Mom had brought back to St. Davids after his death in Brooklyn (he had packed it with a license into the bars that he frequented, and it probably had a history all the way back to Missouri and his banking days). Mom hadn't wanted it around the house and had given it to Jack, who then had taken it with him on a commercial flight back to Colorado—this before the days of hijackings, but even then he had had to give it to the pilot for safekeeping. It was a five-shot top-break, with black hard-rubber grips. I passed it on to Dave, who carefully passed back the Taurus.

"So what do you say? You guys come tomorrow morning, and if I'm up to it, maybe we can go shooting. You like that, Dave? Come around ten. We can have lunch. Your plane doesn't leave until late, right?"

On our way back to the motel, Dave said, "Boy, that Magnum was something else! I love his stories too." Instead of a chore, where he politely went along for my sake, or even out of respect for Jack's illness, he had genuinely enjoyed himself.

The next morning, Jack greeted us and was ready to go. I had no idea where yet. Dave and I climbed into the cab of his Ford V8 pickup. Dave sat in the middle. Jack carried a portable oxygen bottle, just in case. Sometimes, he said, outside like this, he didn't need the oxygen. He was feeling good. He put the oxygen bottle and guns behind the seat. Jan would follow in her car and join us later. He drove the highway north, driving as he always drove, with total vigilance and comprehension, in charge of his machine. After four miles of flat fields, we turned onto a county road, then up a private dirt road of what looked like a farm, with a main house and annex and a gravel parking area, beside which there were picnic tables under a tent roof. This was Great Guns, a private shooting club. "Friends of mine," he said. "Ever since I built that skeet tower for them." He pointed to a skinny, one-hundred foot, steel-girdered tower that stood back off the yard; stabilized by two long cables at each corner and painted bright orange, it looked like a radio tower, or something you would moor a dirigible to. A ladder went up the side. He'd designed the whole thing himself, including the catapults at different levels, which were loaded and controlled electronically from the ground. Surrounding fields stretched out to the horizon.

After introductions to the owner, his wife, and a son a few years older than Dave, all of whom were glad to see Jack and asked how he was feeling; and after we had visited the annex office, where they gave us earplugs, the son took his own pump-action 12 gauge and a box of shells and led Dave and me to a shooting stand, which resembled a garden arbor, just down from the tower. Meanwhile, Jack and the owner settled at a picnic table to watch. The son loaded five shells, and had me push a button on a corded controller, which launched a clay pigeon from the tower behind us; he led it in his sights and blam!—it shattered into powder. He demonstrated for us several times, ejecting a shell each time he cocked the slide, and hitting every pigeon. As he reloaded, he told me he'd won prizes for his marksmanship. He offered the shotgun to Dave and showed him how to tuck the cushioned stock to his shoulder, and lead the target as it flew. Dave did well, three out of five, although he was surprised by the recoil (later, he'd complain that his shoulder was bruised). They both insisted I try as well; I hit a few of the high-flying pigeons, but none of the ones thrown bouncing from hidden traps and meant to simulate rabbits.

We went back to the shaded tables, where Jan had arrived and sat with Jack as he loaded his handguns. The owner was there too. "You like that, Dave? How'd it go?" Jack asked.

"I love it, yeah!"

And the owner's son: "Pretty good shot. He caught on right away."

They had set up a series of knock-down targets about ten yards across the driveway, against bales of hay that served as bullet traps. They were different animal shapes that flipped over, and spinners. "Here you go, Dave, try a handgun."

He gave him the Ruger target automatic that I remembered from St. Davids. Dave held it out in both hands, aimed, and plinked away at the metal rabbits, ducks, rats, and squirrels until he had finished the ten-round clip. He'd hit a few, but did even better next try. We all took turns, including Jan and Jack. Trying out the .22 revolver from last night—hammer cocked, aim, squeeze—I hit four medallions in a row, though my hand trembled and the sight wavered with my breathing each shot. Jack kept reloading. When it was his turn with the Ruger, he shot one-handed and never missed.

Before we started back, Jack went inside the office, and brought back hats for us, one tan, one blue, both with the "Great Guns" insignia, featuring ducks and clay pigeons. Dave chose the blue, and replaced his gray Red Sox cap with it; I slipped on the tan; we both said thanks. We climbed into the pickup; and this time Jack turned on his oxygen bottle and hooked up the tubes and nose clip.

"You should join the NRA back in Boston and follow up with getting Dave into a shooting program," he said.

Without thinking, I laughed. "The NRA? I don't think there is any."

"They have chapters everywhere. Just ask in any gun shop."

"There's that shop we pass in Nonantum," Dave put in.

"We'll look into it," I promised, hoping to sidestep a Second Amendment debate. In Massachusetts, where we had a mandatory one-year sentence for unlawful possession of a firearm, the NRA meant militias, guns stolen from home break-ins, kids with guns, and all the urban woes. I could already imagine Connie's scorn at first sight of our hats, as if we'd turned redneck.

"Seriously. The NRA gets a bum rap from the antis. It's not about irresponsible gun ownership, just the opposite. You can't let the crazies and bad guys ruin it for the rest of us. And you ought to try hunting."

"Well, this sure was a thrill, anyway. Thank you!"

We left it there. Whether or not we joined the gun culture, what counted was Jack's loving, laden gesture of taking Dave shooting, as he had me, a lifetime ago.

Jan made us lunch, with Jack sitting apart again by the open door and hooked up to the oxygen pump. He said it was ironic how he'd come out here originally for his asthma, but what he needed now was oxygen and would do better at sea level. Jan suggested, "Maybe we should buy a self-propelled trailer house. I'll drive it, and we can go touring to Florida." She sounded serious, but he let this go. Their life was in Pierce. He'd served as sheriff for a while, and had been on the board of selectmen for years. He had ideas about fixing the town water supply to support a new housing development. Before we left, he said, "If it wasn't for Jan, I would be dead now. She's all that's keeping me alive." And me: "There are people here who love you, Jack. Hang in there for us. Let's find you the right doctor."

Dave took our picture before we left: Jack, Jan and me, with me reaching behind Jan and giving Jack the traditional devil's horns; Jack is shrunken from his younger 6'1" to 5'8", big-eared, some belly, gray-haired, red crescents under both eyes, a thin grin. He apologized again for avoiding touch: no goodbye hugs.

*

We continued to keep up through emails and occasional phone calls, but now Jan wrote the emails for Jack. He was sick again. The doctor had put him back on steroids. He was seeing a specialist in Greeley next week. I wrote back with news about Ruth, who had been working for a neighborhood center in Boston, and now had won a Fulbright to Colombia for her painting and was about to leave for Bogota; we all worried whether it was safe there, but the Fulbright people had reassured Ruth that it was. Dave had been to Maine with his steady girlfriend and her mom. Later I sent Jack and Jan a digital picture of Ruth taking her leave from Logan Airport, with tears streaming down her face.

The Greeley doctor, Jan wrote, had put Jack on an old-fashioned medicine, uniphyl, which helped, although the side effects were bad. Jan explained that Jack could go without oxygen support for four or five hours; that he maintained well while on steroids, and for a couple of weeks afterwards when first off them. Our visit had been during that two-week window. But his condition had gone downhill from there. The new doctor wanted to stabilize his condition and get him off of steroids, which he would still need to take once or twice a year.

I wrote the news that Ruth was pregnant in Bogota, and was excited, intending to finish out her Fulbright somehow, and deliver in the spring. Marriage was out, we hoped, because the father was the man that Ruth had left in Boston, a kick-boxer and musician, who was older, indigent and unstable, and who had left another child in Norway. We didn't see him as the man for Ruth. We had already accepted his racial difference (part Native-, part African-American). Ruth believed in a multicultural world, and had been brought up with an Asian-American-Jewish-Presbyterian brother (who was also excited by the pregnancy); and we believed with her. But the character of this man was the question.

Jan replied that they too were excited about Ruth and the baby, and that she, Jan, had not thought about a multicultural world for a long time, but liked the thought that it would eliminate any racism in the world. She also wrote that Jack had edema, a possible sign of kidney or heart failure, but after tests, had proved to be okay. She mentioned that she and Jack had become "great jigsaw puzzle fanatics. We usually work one or two a week. It seems to be the only thing that motivates Jack out of bed. He spends at least ninety percent of his time in bed." Promptly, I looked up jigsaw puzzles on the net, and ordered one to be sent to Jack. When they received it, Jan wrote: "I sorted it in the afternoon, and Jack was working on it last night.

It is small, but it is hard. The puzzles have been great for Jack. They not only get him out of bed, they help when he is having anxiety, or cannot sleep. We must have worked at least fifty of them so far this year."

From our side, I passed on more updates about Ruth: that failing to hear back from the baby's father, she had written him a goodbye letter; that she was taking a break from the university to visit a seacoast resort, Cartagena, which was supposedly safe and beautiful; that she had heard the baby's heartbeat, but it was too early to tell yet whether it was girl or boy; that Eva was her choice for a girl's name, but she had no idea for a boy's; that Connie was flying down for January, then again later for the birth and aftermath in April.

About Dave, I wrote that he had invested himself in varsity soccer, where he was a star, and in friendships, and was holding his own in school pretty well; that he was driving responsibly; and that we were applying to some seventeen colleges, including Emerson, though he didn't want to stay in Boston. He was going to visit Ruth in Cartagena for spring break, his first big trip away alone. A good experience for him, Jan said.

When Dave returned, I wrote of my amazement that he had read *Fast Food Nation* there (for lack of TV) and had sworn off of junk food, his staple. Meanwhile, Connie left. Eva was born on April 22. Connie stayed with them until mid-May, returning in time for news of Dave's acceptance by Emerson and for his graduation from Beaver. Ruth and Eva arrived in July and stayed with us until Christmas. Dave moved into his Emerson dorm that September, and our teaching years began again.

Jack and Jan followed all of this, the swirl and complication of our lives like a universe expanding, even as Jack's contracted. They loved the pictures of Eva ("She is beautiful!"). Still, the outlook for Jack continued to be grim, despite Jan's love and care. Judy said she couldn't visit, though she called him often. Poignantly, Jan wrote that an old pilot friend of Jack's had come over to visit and stayed for hours, and all they talked about was flying and airplanes. "It was wonderful for Jack. It is so difficult for us to get out anymore."

I wasn't surprised by Jan's choked, sobbing, yet matter-of-fact call in August of 2004, that "Your brother is gone." He'd been in an accident and hit a tree, she said. He'd seemed fine that morning, had told her that he was taking out the truck to charge the battery, and not to come along. He'd said he'd be right back.

I didn't press her for details; nor did the local authorities or his fellow townsmen. Everyone honored and granted his passing. Judy and I, of course (and surely Jan herself, though she's never spoken outright about it), suspect that his death was deliberate. After four years' ordeal, Jack would have had enough. Bedridden, at best he had a few good hours each day. He lived in constant fear of germs. He had no shop, no dream; no airplane; he was no use around the house; he seldom saw friends; he had no hope of getting better. The more he clung to Jan, the more he must have felt that he was suffocating her, even as his illness robbed him of strength and breath. He wanted her free. If suicide by gun ever tempted him, he'd ruled it out; but with an accident, there'd be no problem with life insurance and there'd be less guilt for Jan. We'll never know for sure. Dave himself rejects this version. He thinks that Jack blacked out or had a coughing fit. The tree in those relatively treeless flatlands just happened to be there. The former race car driver, the pilot, the master mechanic and inventor, the rescuer of others always (as I saw him) had simply lost control and the acceleration surged.

4. Make Love, Not War

A month before Dave graduated from Beaver, the Newton Police had called me on my day off from teaching. "Is this DeWitt Henry?" Yes. "This is Sergeant Manahan. Do you own a 2002 black Acura RSX, Mass. license 16JR36?" Yes. "Has it been operated by an Asian gentleman?" Yes, that's my son, David. "Does he own a gun?" No. "Well, we have a complaint. He was in an altercation on Route 9 with two gentlemen in another car over right of way at a stop sign. Words were exchanged and they claim that he threatened them with a pistol." No, I said. He owns a cap gun, that's all. "Where is he now? Can you put him on the phone?" No, he's still not back from school. "This is a serious matter, Mr. Henry. These gentlemen thought it was a real gun. They took down his license number and came right to the station and made a complaint. What if they'd had a real gun and fired back in self-defense? Then we'd have a tragedy. They were scared. It doesn't matter if it was a toy or not, if a person believes they're being threatened with a gun, it's still a felony. Your son needs to understand that. He could go to jail." I'll talk to him, I said. "No, we won't prosecute. But he needs to call me. I want to give him a good scare." Yes, sir, I said. Thank you. I'll have him call as soon as he gets home.

This was Dave's last episode involving any sort of gun. He hadn't even been the one to wave the gun, he objected; it had been his pal Ben. These older guys, who were assholes, had been yelling and threatening to beat them up. The cap gun happened to be on the seat, and when Ben waved it at them, the other car backed up and Dave had taken off. However, he did call the Sergeant and listened to his scared-straight lecture, which afterwards he said was bullshit. And he did, with a shrug, surrender the cap gun to me for safekeeping.

*

Other than this incident, guns had faded from Dave's life as dating had come in; in fact, he fared more easily with girls than I ever had. At seventeen, he had let us know that he and his steady girl friend, Emily, were having sex. "Yes, Dad, we use protection. We have had three years of sex ed. at school." His pals paired off with steadies. They had mixed overnights at the houses of absent or permissive parents. He pushed our own parental boundaries. He and Emily would shut themselves in his room to watch a movie on the computer and to cuddle, often falling asleep together, until several times we woke to find that Emily had stayed overnight. Emily was Chinese-American, and her Chinese father had left while her mother had cancer. She and Dave bought each other presents, confided, and argued. In fact, the incident with the Newton Police had occurred after Dave had broken off their two-year romance ("The hardest thing I've ever done") and gone back to hanging out with his unattached male pals.

On our return from the visit with Jack, we hadn't joined the NRA; our Great Guns hats had been stashed away; and Dave, Connie and I, missing family time together, had even gone out to the movies and seen Michael Moore's *Bowling for Columbine*—a response to the Columbine, Colorado, high-school shooting spree (and others since), which Moore blamed on the gun culture. Dave liked the film.

Perhaps his sister's experiences with gun violence also had tarnished the glamour of guns. When still in Boston, she'd been shaken by drive-by shootings in Roxbury, where two or three kids that she worked with on youth art and hip hop projects had been victims. She'd published a poem about the shootings in the newspaper and went on to direct her kids in a hip hop version of *Romeo and Juliet* to help voice their grief. Also at a pool hall in Cambridge, she had witnessed a fight between two guys she knew that ended in a fatal shooting. She'd had to testify against a friend, who went to jail.

*

In the spring of his junior year, he had asked us to take him out for dinner to talk about colleges. Emily had come along. As we went over the colleges, he was adamant about a big university as opposed to Emerson, where he'd be near home and tuition was free, and I wanted to know why. I thought maybe sports, but he said no, he didn't want to play college sports. I granted that big universities had a wide variety of programs, but argued that they were impersonal and gave no real attention from the teachers. He said that he had thought this all out. He wanted a 20,000+ campus, in warm weather and with diversity. He had chosen University of Northern Florida off the Tuition Exchange list. We talked about SATs. In bed that night, I said to Connie that I was really proud of him. That this was like his bar mitzvah, his coming of age. We were speaking and listening reasonably; we were out in public, as if on a double date.

*

In private, or at least in private from us, he worked to control his temper by exercising with weights, by understanding the good intentions of others, and hardest for him (I felt) accepting a world of accidental wrongs, where no one was to blame. I was astonished one day, driving him to the airport, when we were stuck in traffic and it looked like we would miss his plane. A younger David would have raged at me, or gotten out of the car, or thrown his CD player out the window. But Dave relaxed. So be it (and we did make it with minutes to spare). He moderated his drinking and smoking weed, at least at home. He still played his hip hop music up loud. He still dressed homeboy style. He was still a TV addict of sports, cooking shows, and movies. He still put off homework until the last minute and then got through it in a rush. He still kept vampire hours. He seemed at war with time, either fighting obligatory matters, or blaming the world (and us) for being too slow, when it came to things he wanted.

*

Soon after his 18th birthday, he got his tattoo, amended now to celebrate his sister's baby. In lines of script, which he'd designed on his computer, it read: "Eva Beauty. Family Love at / First Sight Love Devotion Life / Death Friendship Trust Faith / Forever Loss RIP Gabriel." The birth of Eva had helped to balance his score: Eva as mixed race; Eva as out of wedlock; Eva as Ruth's commitment. All this was healing; as a family we meant this. I imagine him at school, or later in college, and the tattoo as his statement about who he is.

By then, Ruth and Eva were back from Colombia and living with us, though after two months, she had tried reconnecting with the baby's father, gotten a job, a car, and an apartment in Jamaica Plain. For his college application essay, Dave wrote about his Cartagena trip (accompanied by a collage of pictures he had taken there), and largely on the basis of this, he was accepted by the University of Miami and the University of Arizona, but without tuition exchange; and then also by Emerson. He hadn't expected to get into Emerson, and worried that it was too hard; but he did agree to go, on the condition that we buy him his dream car right away, since he'd be saving us so much money. Hence the Acura RSX, with its sun roof, spoiler, and leather seats, better than any car we had ever owned.

*

Dave's freshman year was bumpy. He was put on probation after his first semester, and we feared that he would be suspended, lose heart and self-esteem, and have to attend a community college before reapplying to Emerson. Fortunately he made the choice to buckle down. He tried doses of Ritalin during deadlines. He started working closely with an advisor he trusted, who helped him to avoid lecture classes and had him change his major from Film to Marketing, with a Photography minor. If he studied, he discovered, he could make Bs, and even sometimes an A (a revelation to him). Later, he took summer courses to make up for his freshman Fs.

Meanwhile he thrived socially. He said he loved Emerson. His life there was as independent as if he were thousands of miles away. He quickly made friends. He joined a fraternity, Phi Alpha Beta, where his brothers became "like family." Peer networking led to his finding helpful roommates and off-campus apartments. In junior year, when he lived in a basement apartment in Back Bay, I would stop by on my way home from class to pick up or drop off his laundry; or I would pick him up for medical appointments. He was vice president of his fraternity then, and often busy with meetings. He worked in a nearby tanning salon. Senior year, he moved to the North End, and worked at a liquor store and then a toy store. He spoke of his possessions as "his life." He had a new queen-sized bed. A desk. His wardrobe of prized clothes, coats, and shoes. He had his Apple laptop. His sound system. His TV. His posters. His books. At the end of each year, I would pack it all home, where we stored it in our unused dining room (box spring and mattress leaned against one wall); then come fall, I would load up my hatchback and make several trips to a new apartment. Of course, he had no use for his car, and to save the insurance, we took off the plates and stored it in our driveway. For a while, I put it up for sale for him, but thanks to its tainted "salvage" title, I couldn't find a worthwhile offer. He was happy to get around the city on my bike, or to rent Zip cars as needed. After three more years, I ended up buying it from him myself.

One of his roommates lived in Hawaii (Kona), and for the summer after sophomore year invited him to live there for free and work for his father's landscaping company. The job helped to pay for his tickets. After junior year, he went to a photography institute in Panama, and then to Boulder, Colorado, where he stayed with his former Beaver pal, Ben, and worked at an auto parts store. Travel broadened his perspectives.

Life was never simple, for him, or for us. He remained close with Ruth, who, after a difficult stretch of trying therapy and couples counseling, had given up on the baby's father, and found a new apartment and roommate, and then returned to Colombia after she had saved enough money, in June of his junior year. I remember him coming home one Christmas and going for our traditional visit to the Farrens, with whom we exchanged gifts. Glenda, the mother, always saw him as Gabriel might have been, as did Gabe's adult sisters, Jesse and Caitlin, both of whom had had troubled teen years. Caitlin showed him her album of pictures about Gabe; and looking slowly through them, Dave first said it was "very emotional," and then he began openly to sob and cry. This was a side that he had rarely shown to us; or shown to me, at least.

He dated regularly, but nobody steady until senior year, when he met Katie. As I came out of the library one day, he surprised me on a sidewalk crowded with students, "Hey, Dad!" He wore his stylish shades, and a girl was with him. He introduced us, but I missed her name and thought she was someone else he had mentioned, one of his friends' girls. He ribbed me about this later, when Connie and I took them out for dinner in the North End. Katie shared an apartment several blocks down from Dave's. She was ambitious, beautiful, and bright. A journalism major, she hoped to be an anchor on TV news. She had already acted in movies in Hong Kong, where she lived, and where her Irish-American father was a professor in film studies at the Chinese University of Hong Kong. She had a younger brother. Her mother had separated from her father and lived in the Philippines.

Dave traveled with her to London that March, where they stayed with her friends. After graduation, we sponsored his travel to Hong Kong for the summer. Her father helped him find an internship at *The Hollywood Reporter Asia* and put him up for three months in their home. We followed his progress as best we could by international cell phone calls. Katie helped to reinforce and to normalize his Asian roots. The racism he once told us he had experienced "every day" at Beaver appeared provincial in this worldly view. Dave had also been impressed by an older classmate, a Korean adoptee, who traveled to Seoul to search for his birth parents and had made a documentary film about the trip. Even before hearing this, Connie had promised him his own trip to Seoul for a graduation present, perhaps as part of an organized program. But now from Hong Kong, first he and Katie took a side trip to Thailand, and then he visited Seoul alone. He managed it all despite the language barrier. Always as taciturn as Conrad's Captain McWhirr, he had little to share afterwards except that everyone took him for Korean and expected him to understand Korean when they spoke to him.

Meeting Jack and shooting probably had no real impact on David's coming of age; but to my mind, the transformation began there and grew in gradual stages from first love, driver's license, Eva's birth, tattoo, first car, graduation from Beaver, acceptance by Emerson, life at college, roommates, summer work and travel, mature love and then his college graduation. One of my proudest moments as a parent was to stand up as a faculty member in my academic robe, announce his name in the microphone, and embrace him in his academic robe before he started across the stage to receive his degree. I wish Jack could have seen it. Hugs, in fact, became his specialty: in thanks, in parting, as his manly gesture of emotion, like sports hugs. "Love ya, Dad." And the feel of his lean, solid, muscular back and shoulders would gladden me.

Father of the Bride

At 67, I hadn't travelled much and only knew a few Spanish phrases, but here I was on my way from Boston to Cartagena, Colombia. The second and final sabbatical of my teaching career. And my daughter Ruth at 31 was getting married. Her life had brought me here. Fortunately I was traveling with my 23-year-old son, who was a seasoned traveler. He lived with his girl friend in the North End and worked at a service agency for the elderly. My wife, Connie, on leave from her job, had flown down a week earlier. I'd never met the groom, Diego Torres, who only spoke Spanish. All I knew was that he and Ruth had fallen in love while they were both living at the Bella Vista hotel in Cartagena. When Ruth visited home with us last summer, she'd kept in contact on the computer and cell phone. We'd heard their laughter, his voice interwoven with hers. I'd seen his picture: younger than she, handsome, lean and muscular, wearing a ponytail. He was studying for an undergraduate degree in history at the university in Cartagena. He was from Bogota. Connie had met him and said that he "got" Ruth; that this was serious, and that he was loving with our granddaughter Eva. More easy-going than ambitious, he subsisted on an assistantship at the university and also by selling jewelry that he made. Ruth earned some money from teaching an American Civilization course at the university.

More family and friends would fly in tomorrow: Connie's younger brother Ray and his wife Barbara from Washington; Ruth's close friend from Boston, Elexia, and her parents from Texas. Connie's best friend Glenda and her daughter Caitlin were seated farther forward on our flight. Connie had hoped for more family, but her oldest brother, a rabbi, was bespoken, as was her older sister. Ray would speak the rabbi's part at the ceremony.

As we descended, I had a wing-tilted view of the ocean and a peninsula of new high rises, not unlike Miami Beach. We landed safely, taxied to a stop, and the passengers applauded. Doors opened both fore and aft, and gathering our carry-ons and winter coats, we filed out the back down a rickety stair and into the tropical day, ninety degrees, bright, and humid.

Inside the terminal was air-conditioned. We filed through immigration, where the busy official spoke no English, but Dave managed to convey that we were staying at the Bella Vista Hotel for one week, and were visiting for his sister's boda. The official stamped our passports and waved us through. We spotted five-year-old Eva and then Ruth outside the baggage claim cordons, and stopped for hugs and kisses over the ropes. Connie and Diego were outside, Ruth said. We found our bags, managed to clear them through the customs inspections, then exited to the street. Connie looked wonderful. Dave shrugged off his shirt immediately, to his tee shirt. Diego wore a tee shirt and shorts. "What do you think of Colombia, Dad?" Ruth asked. It was beautiful, I said, as exotic as Oz. The flowers in front of the terminal were vivid reds, yellows, pinks, and greens. The air was heavy and sweet. Diego was attentive and busy, taking the bags, ordering and negotiating with two small, air-conditioned cabs.

*

The Bella Vista hotel was a single-story, white stucco compound across the highway from the beach. A steady ocean breeze cooled us. Through ornate barred gates, across a tiled patio, through glass-paned doors: Connie, Ruth and Eva led the way as Dave and I followed with Diego and our luggage. Ruth got our keys at the desk, then led us past a restaurant and down a tiled corridor open to the sky, with doors to rooms on both sides. Connie's and my room was several doors down, just at the point where the corridor opened into a courtyard shaded by three ancient rubber trees, whose interlocking canopies created shade. The floor throughout was paved with reddish tiles. Potted plants and flowers lined the walls. David followed Ruth to his own room as Connie unlocked and showed me ours: two regular and one double-decker bunk bed, with thin mattresses on boards. Overhead a ceiling fan turned. There were fixtures with bare light bulbs on the far wall. A closet alcove by the front window. In the bathroom, no toilet seat. The shower was a pipe out of the wall without a shower head. Toilet paper went into a waste basket instead of being flushed. The wiring and plumbing all seemed makeshift. "This is the way here. Now, don't complain," Connie warned, although she worried that Ray and Barbara would see Bella Vista as squalid rather than charming, especially if they visited Ruth and Diego's apartment. They themselves had booked a five-star hotel in the center of Cartagena's Old City.

I changed into shorts, tee shirt and running shoes. We crossed the courtyard and headed through a passageway to the back of the compound, which faced a parking lot. To the left were mops, buckets, ladders and a stone sink where two maids washed sheets. To the right, a broken sidewalk, and two doors down, Eva appeared behind an open screen door. "Hi, Nana." Then a boy came out behind her. Connie said, "*Hola,* Theo," as they dashed around us. He was Eva's playmate, and his father, I would later learn, was an expatriate American painter, Tim, who had lived for twenty years with his Colombian wife in the only second-story apartment, somewhere on the other side of the courtyard.

Here, Ruth and Diego's single room had a mattress on the floor for them, and behind some bookcases and shelving, another for Eva; art and hangings on the walls; a small table with chairs; a hanging lamp and overhead fan. Diego sat making jewelry, drinking a beer and talking with two friends. They stood and shook hands. They were all soccer fans and presumably classmates. The taller, Flako, knew some English and asked about my teaching and college. We stammered together in good will, but soon gave up. Connie helped Ruth in the cramped kitchen, making salad, tofu, rice and beans. We carried the plates and bowls of food, pitchers of juice, and glasses out and around to the courtyard tables, and were joined there by Dave, by Glenda and Caitlin, and Eva, Diego and his friends. I watched and tried to make a connection with Diego, whose good humor and alertness impressed me. He had to juggle the agendas of his own family and friends, as well as Ruth's, while balefully acknowledging the difficulties in getting to know each other.

However stressed, Ruth herself was radiant, tan and healthy. She and Connie had been planning the wedding for the past week, but still had loose ends to resolve. The ceremony was to be held at Playa Blanca, an island paradise that Ruth and Diego had taken Connie to see on an earlier trip. We would need bathing suits. I knew that Ruth had scripted a ceremony that would suit Diego's Catholic family as well as her own Judaism; and that she had many friends coming, including the youths she worked with in the barrio. On budget, she, Connie, and Diego worried about getting liquor from Diego's local contacts wholesale. They worried about the wedding cake, when and how to pick it up. They worried about prices for two or three special buses to take all of us to the island. They worried about the wedding dinner. Diego wanted fish with the eyes still in, which repulsed Connie, but apparently was a custom here. On his cell phone, Diego was trying to make reservations.

Ruth and Connie told me to relax; enjoy myself. Teaching was off my mind. I had a book to read, my notebook, and Connie's laptop for email, thanks to a wireless connection that worked best in the courtyard. I could take Eva across the highway to the beach; or I could sprawl on our bed with her friends and watch *The Wizard of Oz*—our favorite movie, which I had brought along in DVD with English with Spanish subtitles. There were gaps of time. Within the larger, and threatening mystery of Colombia and Cartagena, I adjusted to Bella Vista as my reality for now, enclosed, sheltered, and with family nearby.

*

Ruth had stayed here on her first visit to Cartagena from Bogotá during her Fulbright time. She had described the hotel as a kind of arts colony, well known within the world of Cartagena artists. Many people had lived here for years, paying monthly rent and then packing their stuff up come December to make room for the tourists whose money kept the hotel afloat for the rest of the next year, after which the regulars returned to their rooms. Ruth had helped Enrique, the owner, to organize an arts festival here. According to Tim, who introduced himself to me in the courtyard, Enrique was a misanthrope who hated people but was sentimental about cats: hence the scores of cats, which yowled and mated on the tile roofs and otherwise had run of the place.

*

Connie's first visit had been during Ruth's pregnancy. They had wandered up the beach to swim and been threatened by teen-aged delinquents with knives, who despite Ruth's blistering rebukes in Spanish ("I'm pregnant! This is my mother! Have you no shame?") took Connie's wedding ring. In my office at school, I looked with mixed pride and puzzlement at the photographs Connie had brought back from then: Ruth pregnant and pear-shaped, standing in front of the Bella Vista colonnade; and again, at the seawall, with the ocean behind her. I also kept other pictures of her departure from Boston, her tears at the airport gate when she had said goodbye. She'd had no idea then that she was pregnant. She had left her life in Boston, where she had been living some distance from us in an apartment with friends in Jamaica Plain, including the musician-and-kickboxer, with whom she had broken up, and who was Eva's father. I remember when Ruth called from Colombia to tell us the news and her decision to have the baby. Connie had been instantly supportive. Ruth had written to the father, Khari; and Connie had tracked him down through his Sensei in Roxbury, to whom she delivered the news and Ruth's emailed letters. Khari never replied. I had written to Ruth myself: "The dad in me—not of scoldings, but of wanting the most for you—partly wishes you had seriously planned your baby in better circumstances, but there is no partly about trusting your choice now; and being excited with you about the adventure of a new life. I love you and the missions of your life, which now are incarnated, the right word."

Connie had shared Ruth's letters for Khari with me. He was three years older than Ruth. He had been born and raised in the Piano Factory, a Boston artists' community. His mother had been a jazz vocalist, African dancer, and ballet teacher. He'd never known his own father, who'd been sent to prison when Khari was a baby and had died there. Khari had been to Norway, where supposedly he had been a champion kickboxer, and where he'd fathered a son, Fury, then fled. His mother now had had a stroke and lived alone in a facility in Fall River, while Khari himself was homeless and was always couch-surfing. He had no formal education. He didn't want to work, because any sort of regular work, like family, would compromise his dojo training and his music career. As a hip hop performer, "Bambu," he had his local following, went from gig to occasional gig, and hoped for a commercial recording that would make him a star. Physically, he was a bearish man, glad-handing, and had a rolling, lumbering walk, as if keeping balance on a shifting deck. He prided himself on his mixed Native American and African-American heritage and attended pow wow gatherings in central Massachusetts and on the Cape.

I had first met him in Ruth's bed. Connie had mentioned that Ruth was dating such a person, but otherwise I had had no warning. Connie had enlisted me to help move Ruth out of her apartment in Jamaica Plain back to our house, where we would store her things after she left for Colombia. Ruth had let us in. Her room—one of five or six—had a double mattress on the floor, covered with rumpled quilts. She had clothes on hangers and in garbage bags. And all sorts of paintings, big ones, on an easel, and others propped against the wall. Since it was crowded without chairs, as Connie stood by and Ruth finished dressing, I sat on the bed, when I felt a bump and something underneath me moving. This proved to be Khari, who mumbled something, got up and exited in his boxers. Although we'd resisted Ruth's departure to Colombia, Fulbright or no, we were glad she was leaving Khari behind.

As soon as news of her pregnancy reached him through friends, he withdrew. He did call her finally, only once, and after she'd already determined to move on without him. He didn't know where he'd be living from month to month, and didn't have a phone of his own. To his grandiose vows that he would move to Colombia, build a house, and "everything would work out lovely," she wrote to him that he was all talk, no action. Nonetheless, she imagined his fears. She would not, like his son's mother in Norway, make financial ultimatums (he would never see his son until he paid support). Ruth thought this new challenge deepened the wound of breaking with his son: "I think how powerless you must feel." He had told her once that "family and music were of necessity two separate and different roads." But now the path seemed natural to her, and either he came along or she'd need to let go. In that case, he would have to figure out on his own what he wanted to do and how active he wanted to be in their child's life. Friends told her to quit theorizing, look at his actions; the actions spoke for themselves.

When ultrasound revealed the fetus to be a girl, she decided on the name Eva, a family name she had promised to use years before to Nana Hazel (Connie's mother) on her deathbed.

*

During her pregnancy, she'd stayed with Fulbright friends in Bogota and taken art courses. Despite the baby, she had decided to live out her Fulbright year and deliver it there. Then for a week's vacation, she had taken another grantee's advice, and headed for Cartagena. At Bella Vista, she met Eva Maria, "a young dreamer with bright blue contacts that shocked against the cinnamon of her skin." Eva Maria "gave workshops on how to run a community radio" in an impoverished barrio on the city's outskirts. She and Ruth talked about hip hop and Eva Maria invited her to the barrio to meet some young MCs (rappers). On the way, Eva Maria told her about "social cleansing" in the barrio by a vigilante group that killed fifteen-year-old troublemakers, and when Ruth arrived she found a newly posted sign with 36 names warning them to leave immediately or be killed. As Ruth and the MCs shared rhymes later, the youths free-styled about the list, about the links between the vigilantes and the police, and about their own refusal to keep quiet. The experience shook her.

In post civil-war Guatemala, five years before this, Ruth had had a spiritual vision about evil that connected with her awakening to the Holocaust and her Jewish heritage. In her own words: "I'd swallowed the stories of massacre survivors, visions of mass graves exhumed in a pile of small haunting bones. Then swigged them down with history books that outlined my own country's role in the genocide of 700 indigenous villages, razed to the ground in the name of cheap bananas." The social cleansing in Colombia made her wonder "What was my homeland financing now"?

Hip hop and its protest became her calling. She had connected with MCs from Cartagena at a drum festival, and heard about LaHeroiK, a hip hop movement that brought together some 50 artists to meet regularly in the Cartagena library. At five months pregnant, she decided to move there permanently and have her baby. Bit by bit, she joined the "hip hop family" of LaHeroiK. A woman singer, Petrona Martinez, was recording her album in the patio of Bella Vista, and Ruth induced labor by dancing to the drums. Connie made her second trip to help her through the birth, and was with her for the delivery, April 22, 2003, as I had been with her for Ruth's. My first sight of Eva would be at Logan airport in June. I'd be a grandfather suddenly, and smitten.

*

Ruth and the baby stayed in our second bedroom, with David downstairs, and we helped out, while busy with our teaching lives and parenting David through his college-seeking senior year. Ruth bought a car and (as she wrote later) "became an open mic fiend, spitting whenever I could get the chance, scribbling verses on napkins at the jazz bar where I worked nights." She also started seeing Khari again, though he offered nothing in terms of support for the baby.

To Connie and me, Ruth's immersion in hip hop seemed like an ideological maelstrom. We were dedicated teachers, who had struggled for a middle-class life. But to Ruth and her friends, some of whom were anti-Semitic, we were enemies of the Revolution. Not that Khari and the hip hoppers walked the walk of urban guerrillas, but they reveled in talking—or chanting—the talk. We attended Ruth's first big performance as "Mama Rut" at the Jorge Hernandez Center in the South End. Connie had slipped inside to watch, leaving me to tend the carriage with Eva in the vestibule where the noise was muted. But after a series of other hip hoppers, Ruth took the stage. As she started her polemical chants, Eva's eyes popped open. What am I doing here? Where is this? Who are you? Recognized me. I tried to keep Eva from crying as her mom's amplified voice shouted through the walls, followed by applause.

Through a poet and vocalist who was also a new mother, Ruth found work in a middle-school program. Then her Guatemalan former college roommate helped her get a job bartending nights at Wally's, a downtown jazz bar. Before long, she and Eva moved into an apartment in Jamaica Plain with Khari. I remember the complicated drive to get there and going up rickety backstairs to the third floor. The bedroom had a slanting ceiling with a skylight that Khari had borrowed my drill to fix. They put in the crib for Eva, and they had a mattress on the floor. They invited us for dinner. I remember his karate stick leaning by the stove. He took Ruth and the baby out busking at the nearby T stop, performing raps and begging. He went from one free food event to another, and occasionally stole from Bread and Circus as his "protest for indigenous land being stolen."

After Ruth's complaints that Khari didn't work and couldn't pay rent; after she had traveled to New York; and after she had been exhausted from putting on an art show, I answered our phone and Khari told me to come get Ruth, that "she needed blood kin." He repeated that. Connie rushed to get her and the baby, while I stayed home with David. When Connie returned with Ruth, Ruth was tripping, as if on acid, glassy-eyed and spewing nonsense. Connie called Glenda, who was a social worker, and Glenda came over and tried talking gently with Ruth; then told us to call Boston Lying-In. Ruth needed sedation. Again I stayed home. Ruth was admitted to the mental ward for a "psychotic episode." Connie was distraught and I was sick with worry, convinced that the extremes Ruth was trying to link, all of them and so many, had simply broken her.

She was there for more than a week. We visited her with Eva for Thanksgiving, down a corridor to a locked door, with a doorbell, a thick window and wire mesh. Glenda had made us a basket with plates, cups, silverware, apple juice, turkey slices, gravy, and stuffing, which I carried. A nurse led us to a library, where we found Ruth in her hospital robe and talking to a younger girl-patient. Ruth hugged each of us and took Eva in her arms, weeping; then introduced the girl, who had become her friend (an attempted suicide, Ruth later told us). We invited the girl to our dinner, but she excused herself. The nurse then showed us to a room with a metal table and chairs. We crowded in. Connie put out the table cloth and dishes. We joked about how wretched and wonderful a Thanksgiving it was, and Ruth seemed to be herself again, although they didn't release her for another few days.

She and Eva moved back home with us. She continued taking her meds, then skipped by accident, then on purpose. She didn't like the way they made her feel. Otherwise, she was taking things one step at a time. Khari wanted to keep the apartment, but since he couldn't pay for it, she gave the landlady notice. She and Khari went to family counseling sessions together, but then he quit.

Into the new year, Ruth grew restive. Eva turned two that April. To us, Eva was the reincarnation of Ruth; and in a flood of feeling, she brought back our early love and our parenting. When Ruth found another job, we took Eva on weekends, and her married friend Jesse took her Tuesday nights while Ruth bartended at Wally's. She also arranged for Eva's daycare near the Hernandez Center weekdays. She mounted an art show at a Jamaica Plain cafe where she sold paintings and performed her songs.

She found a new apartment with a woman roommate. She wanted to keep Khari in Eva's life, so we invited him and his mother to our house for big holidays. Khari had never given Ruth anything, beyond "little bits here and there" for Eva's support. He'd never bought Eva anything. But he would come blustering in, all family; big glad-hand and hug for me. He would bring friends, and if we had liquor out, offer it bountifully: "Mi casa, your casa," he told them, while I stiffly went along. I'd ask about his music, how was it going? And he'd reply, "Great, great! Things are coming round! Got an album out soon!" Ruth later wrote about this time: "Since we had fallen apart, he'd seen Eva less and less. His long absences outweighed his all-too-occasional presence in her life."

Running an inner-city youth arts program, she staged a hip hop version of Romeo and Juliet with her students after a twelve-year-old friend of theirs was shot. Senseless violence was commonplace in their neighborhoods, and they wore pins of remembrance on their hats. "Some kids have five, six pins on their hats," she wrote, "and you cringe on the subway at the smoothness of their young faces against the tragedy they carry in their heads." When one of her most talented teens was shot and killed, the evil of it seared her as deeply as witnessing the Guatemalan death pit. The boy's older sister became Ruth's friend. "She was a mother whose own home became a community center in a neighborhood that desperately needs one."

In time she saved enough from her work and paintings to move back to Cartagena, with Eva. Before the move, she'd gone each year for brief visits, but when Eva was four, she took a leave and went down to organize a cultural exchange between the hip hop community there and the community in Boston. Kids there wrote letters back and forth with kids in Boston and sent pictures. She did workshops and translated lyrics. She also met Diego on that trip.

She returned to Boston, determined to settle in Cartagena and make a life. She finished up her job and moved to Bella Vista that summer. She was thirty. I worried for her, and for Eva, just coming to school age. I was at a loss for how and why my daughter would disappear into a life that I had no way to imagine or identify with. Connie, on the other hand, rose wonderfully to all Ruth's and David's occasions. She learned Spanish, bit by bit. She visited Cartagena on her vacation. She used the computer for international calling, and kept in close touch. Then one night, come fall, Ruth announced on Skype that she was engaged, at which Connie whooped, wept and was triumphant, while I was unsure what to feel.

*

In Boston, as Eva had grown from toddler to school age, I had loved playing with her. I read to her, at night, until she fell asleep; I cuddled and watched TV with her. She had the habit of getting into bed with Connie and me during the night, and kicking my back. Ruth had asked what I wanted to be called, and with irony, I had said, "Grandee." So Eva would have Grandee fixations. She insisted on following me around, and sharing whatever preoccupied me. Now at Bella Vista, she still had school; she slept with us, and I woke at 6:15 to Connie getting her dressed and fed, then walking her to school. At 2 p.m., Connie left again to walk her home. Afternoons, Dave and I took Eva across the highway to the beach, where we bucked and rode the waves. I was surprised by how well she had adapted to life here: to the language, culture, and lifestyle. Diego was her longed-for Poppa. Charlito was her boyfriend and confederate.

Ray and Barbara invited us for lunch: Connie, me, Dave, Ruth and Diego, while Eva was at school. This was my own first look at the Old City, with its high fortress walls, tunnel-like entrance, and narrow, cobbled streets. We and Ray had been close since the first years of our marriage, while he was at Boston University. He was a corporate lawyer now, and his wife was a former journalist; they had two nearly-grown daughters. Our mini-cabs left us off at the entrance to their hotel, which had been converted from a 17th-century monastery and faced the main square. We called from the front desk, he and Barbara came down, and we walked the colorful streets with them in search of the perfect restaurant, preferably air-conditioned. At the one we found, we ate around a long table, with Ray at the head and Barbara at the foot. Ray asked Ruth obvious questions that I had never managed to ask. How had Ruth and Diego met? Ruth translated the question, then told her version in English, with Diego smiling and trying to follow.

They'd met at Bella Vista, where he lived while taking classes and working at the university. They had started talking in the patio. Then one night a friend had offered to take Eva for a sleepover. Ruth, looking to take advantage of a rare night out, saw Diego and asked: would he like to go salsa dancing that night? That is, if he didn't mind her being a single mother, with a four-year-old? (Like her mother, Ruth loves dancing, especially salsa dancing; and gets all fluid and sexy, flaunting her body, telling her story of gladness and daring.) Eva had picked him as well, and told Ruth to marry him.

Was Diego adopting Eva? Ray asked. Had they looked into it? Would they need the biological father's permission? He wouldn't be a problem, Ruth said. He had no claim. His name wasn't on the birth certificate, and the laws were different in Colombia.

Friday's pre-wedding party dinner was held in a cafe near Bella Vista. Earlier that day, Diego's mother, Carmenza, and his two sisters had arrived from Bogota, and we had traded "Mucho gustos," but they didn't attend. Diego's father, Omar, had divorced her, moved to Cartagena, and married and had children with another woman. Diego and his father were still close, Ruth explained; but his parents were estranged. Otherwise, the families and Ruth's and Diego's combined friends, some thirty of us, became acquainted, while food, music, drink and dancing helped to bridge the language barrier. I met his father. And with Ruth translating, back and forth, I told him that I was proud of our joining families. He was younger than I was, balding, a little stockier and shorter, but strong. When I tried jokingly to compliment Colombian weed, he frowned and grew serious. *That's not what you should think of when you think of Colombia.* Then he asked what religion was I? Protestant, I said. Ruth translated this as *humaniste,* and he nodded. Who knows what he thought about Ruth, her age, her school-age daughter, her politics and her art? He must have worried about support; or that Diego might move to America. On both sides, there was troubled goodwill. We promised: I would learn more Spanish before my next visit, and he, more English.

*

The air-conditioned bus for the wedding party loaded at Bella Vista at 7 a.m. Saturday morning. I had no idea how long the trip to this island was, but we all showed up, however bleary-eyed, carrying our special changes of clothes, shoes, and bathing suits in backpacks, and climbed aboard. The luggage bay of the bus was full of supplies. Diego and his friends had skin bladders of wine, which they squirted into their mouths. I took a window seat with Connie beside me and Eva and Charlito across from her. Ray and Barbara were farther front, as were Dave, Glenda, Caitlin, Ruth and Diego. We were underway. A second bus would leave a few hours later for wedding guests, primarily Ruth's hip hop friends. The wedding was scheduled for 2 p.m.

*

Stop, start, turn, we made our way through the outskirts of Cartagena, past oil refineries, past hardscrabble businesses and their clamoring signs—auto repair, knife sharpening, video rental—down a turn-off to the ferry landing, where our bus parked behind some pickups, motorbikes, bikes, and cars. An air horn signaled to the barge across the waterway, which then slowly made its way back to our landing, docked, and we were waved on, packed tightly bumper to bumper. The barge backed off, swung, and crept steadily towards the other landing. When our bus eased off at last, I thought, fine, this is the island, we're almost there.

We headed inland on a paved road, but soon the paving gave way to dirt. And for what seemed another hour, I braced myself on the armrests in mid air, attempting to ride the jolts, lurches, sways, slams, and dips. My back seized. I was sure we'd break an axle. The driver did his best, in first gear, but the ordeal went on and on. Dust rose everywhere. The landscape could have been African: the earth in drought; people in scattered tin or thatched-roofed shelters; starved dogs; groups of odd-looking cattle with humped backs and dewlaps. Still, Connie assured me, the place we were headed was beautiful, I'd see. You could also get there by boat, she explained, but the sea voyage was rough. Then she told me, low and in my ear as the bus swayed, that Ruth and Diego were already married. One of their errands had been to get married on Wednesday, at a civil ceremony with Omar and Connie in the town hall. I didn't understand why this was necessary, but it had to do with the legal record, and they didn't want people to know because that would make today's ceremony anticlimactic.

Eventually we turned into a clearing, with fences and dust-coated, parched trees, and parked. Nearby, an odd cow or bull wandered. The ground was spotted with dung. Led by Ruth, Diego and the others, we shouldered our backpacks, duffel bags, and carried anything else, food and all, down a steep rocky gulch. This way! Careful! We stepped from rock to rock. At the bottom, we came out on the beach, which hadn't been visible before: white sand, palm trees, thatch-roofed buildings, tents, and colors everywhere. Water of the purest turquoise merged out to darker shadows where seaweed grew and then to deeper water. A steady breeze gusted off the water. Rollers surged in and broke. Trees, not merely palms, but complex trees like the rubber trees at Belle Vista, framed the view.

*

Ruth and Diego promptly claimed four or five thatched-roof shelters. Under each shelter were several picnic tables, on which we spread paper tablecloths, held down by coconut shells filled with sand. We seemed to have this area of the beach mostly to ourselves. Rentals had been arranged, I assumed. The *Policia* barracks with several uniformed police was nearby, but we couldn't change there, as planned; instead, we had a rickety shack with a storage room for our bags, where the men took turns changing; and on the other side was a changing room for the women and primping. We set up an area for chairs and benches on the edge of the beach rim. Five palm trees became the frame and masts for the huppa wedding canopy that Diego and his father and friends worked on in the whipping wind, tying string to each of the four corners (I recognized it as Ruth's blue silk bedspread), then scaling up each palm trunk to tie the strings taut. An heirloom of lace from Connie's mother also needed to be carefully tied. But eventually there it all was, flapping away like the kite of a hang-glider. Meanwhile, Ray, Dave and I helped gather stacks of plastic chairs from the shelters, and set out fifty in concentric rows, facing the huppa and ocean. No one had eaten yet. The next bus with guests wouldn't arrive for an hour or two.

Dave and I changed into bathing suits and went swimming to kill time. The beach was absolutely beautiful, almost superfluous in beauty. The water was warm, waist- to shoulder-deep as far as I went, with surging breakers. Underfoot was smooth. I had a beatific, idiot smile on my face, basking in it all, although I was alert to the huckster and beggar islanders poised to prey. Ruth had warned us to ignore them. Later, bored with swimming, I sat apart on a log of driftwood and contemplated the vacant ocean and sky. I felt unmoored, my worldliness beyond its ken. I worried for my loved ones, as I lacked language or command. I couldn't communicate with Diego or his family. When Ruth was little, I'd felt estranged as she began to learn the Hebrew Shabbat prayer, a prayer I still couldn't recite. Now this would be her life, and Eva's life. They would visit; I would try to learn Spanish and visit. Connie even spoke of retiring here, which I rejected. I couldn't imagine myself, uprooted from my life and friends in Boston. Would Diego learn English? Would he finish his history degree and become a teacher? Would they move and find work in the States?

I thought of my father, again, at my wedding to Connie, and how he and she had related by debating politics. We'd been married in Hazel's Miami condo, with a pond out back. I thought of him dressed up with Mom and sitting in Hazel's living room, oddly meek and chastened, out of his element, but relieved to see me settling down. I thought of standing with Judge Sweet, Justice of the Peace, at the huppa; of Mozart's *Jupiter* symphony playing; and Connie, whom I hadn't been allowed to see for a week, coming down the stairs and towards me, tanned, radiant, and eyes shining, all in white. I thought of our vows in front of our families. I thought of our passion for each other. I thought of our youth. And of our bravery.

I thought of our shared meaning, despite our differences. How Connie had needed children foremost, while I was scared that I couldn't support a family (a fear too like Khari's, I admit). Then once

Ruth was born, Connie's seeking friends in childcare and political action groups, while my friends were writers. Of our struggle together publishing a literary magazine out of our apartment. Of our infertility ordeal and adopting David as an infant. My father's, then my mother's death. My novel's rejections. My tenure-track hire at Emerson, at last. Connie's hire by the Atrium School, where both Ruth and David went, and her devoting her heart to her teaching as much as I did to the magazine and my teaching. The struggle to balance our time and sacrifice, with rival commitments. Deaths of friends. Hazel's death. The heartaches, losses, and vicissitudes. The adolescent struggles. My own shortcomings, and despair. And through it all, Connie as the driving force, as both my mother and Hazel had been in our pasts.

Now I marveled at Ruth. What an amazing, gifted soul this person was, and how glad I was to know her. She had managed to weave the different strains of her life into something viable and whole, at least for her, and for Eva, who was growing up taking it all for granted. At least I prayed so.

*

Ruth's hip-hop friends arrived from the second bus. We changed into our formal clothes. The women clustered in the recesses of the shack. At our planned starting time, a charter boat arrived and anchored in the idyllic sight-line of our palm tree theater, where Ray had set up the altar. Ray and I thought the boat might be bringing more wedding guests, but as a launch set off from the boat itself, stopped in shallow water, and thirty or so passengers waded to shore, they proved to be weekend trippers. They walked through our site as if it wasn't there, until Ray put up a string to keep them out. An even larger cruise boat anchored as well, and a launch brought those passengers in. Ray waved them around our area.

Connie appeared at last, lovely in a light blue dress and gauze shawl. Ruth emerged from the women's changing room, totally made up, white wedding dress, layered turquoise necklace, and a crown of flowers. The bridesmaids, Lexie, Nadia, and Caitlin and a few others wore full length turquoise dresses. The ushers, among them Dave, and except for Flako (the only usher dressed in a blue soccer shirt), were dressed in long-sleeved white shirts and white pants, and had blue ribbons tied around one arm. Both bridesmaids and ushers wore turquoise necklaces. The colors, royal blue and white, represented Diego's favorite soccer team.

Connie yelled Vamos! to the women for the procession. No music, but Diego had gone to wait at the altar. First came two little girls passing out coral stones; then Eva in her white dress and crown, and Charlito in white shirt and pants, with flowers; then Flako and Caitlin, then Dave and Nadia, and finally us, me on one side and Connie on the other, holding hands with Ruth as she gripped her bouquet, and escorting her to join Diego under the flapping huppa and before the table with candles and wine. Behind the table stood Diego's friend, bearded Mono (a notary public), who would recite his part in Spanish, Glenda, who would recite hers in English, and Ray, his in Hebrew. Meanwhile, weekenders from the boats crowded the periphery. They may or may not have seen other weddings here, but surely never a hybrid ceremony like this. Mono, Ray, and Glenda gave their benedictions and the couple took glasses of wine, made their vows in Spanish and English, face to face, earnest and laughing, swoon kissed, and stomped the traditional glass.

We cast our coral stones for luck into the sea, then headed for the banquet in the shelters. Glasses of wine were poured; plates were brought out by the island preparers, whose cook shack was nearby, each featuring the fish with eyes intact and little teeth, a serving of fried rice, and salad.

Ray came around with a fifth of J&B and poured generous, stinging shots. There were toasts. Connie was off helping. I sat across from Diego's mother and sisters, who only spoke together. Then following more toasts, Ruth and Diego cut the multi-tiered cake and passed around slices.

Diego's boom box began blasting reggae. Ruth sought me out, took my hand, and pulled me out into the sunlight, where we danced barefoot, against a surround of palm trees, the tents of campers, and the turquoise ocean and cloudless sky: just us, at first, the bride and father of the bride. We were a story to strangers. A story to in-laws, family, and friends. A story to Barbara, who captured our picture. Stories defy time, of course, with their ever-afters. Who knows what will come? But here, arms stretched out, holding hands, ducking and swinging to the beat, we filled our moment with belief.

Acknowledgements

"On Golf" appeared in *Wilderness House Literary Review;* "Father of the Bride" and "Perspectives" appeared in *Solstice: A Magazine of Diverse Voices;* "Deaths in My Life" was adapted from the Introduction to *Sorrow's Company: Writers on Loss and Grief* (Beacon Press) and appeared in *Memoir;* "Embodiment" appeared in *Nerve;* "Long-Distance" appeared in *Juked;* "Swimming" appeared in *Ducts;* a section of "Guns in My Life" appeared as "Jack's Last Ride" in *Del Sol Review.* I am grateful to these editors and publications.

About the Author

DeWitt Henry was the founding editor of *Ploughshares.* He has published a novel, two memoirs, a story collection, and several anthologies, as well as *Sweet Marjoram,* a collection of notes and essays. He is a Professor Emeritus at Emerson College and serves as a contributing editor to both *Woven Tale Press* and *Solstice* magazines. For details see dewitthenry.com.

Manufactured by Amazon.ca
Bolton, ON